Teaming with Opportunity

Teaming with Opportunity

Media Programs, Community Constituencies, and Technology

Lesley S. J. Farmer

2001
Libraries Unlimited
A Division of Greenwood Publishing Group, Inc.
Englewood, Colorado

LIBRARIES UNLIMITED
A Division of Greenwood Publishing Group, Inc.
P.O. Box 6633
Englewood, CO 80155-6633
1-800-237-6124
www.lu.com

Library of Congress Cataloging-in-Publication Data

Farmer, Lesley S. J.
    Teaming with opportunity : media programs, community constituencies, and technology / Lesley S.J. Farmer.
        p. cm.
    Includes bibliographical references and index.
    ISBN 1-56308-878-9
    1. School libraries--Activity programs--United States. 2. Media programs (Education)--United States. 3. Information literacy--Study and teaching--United States. 4. Internet in education--United States. 5. Community and school--United States. 6. Curriculum planning--United States. I. Title.

Z675.S3 F2378 2001
027.8'0973--dc21

2001029827

Dedicated to some of my partners in education:
Tamalpais Union High School District
California State University, Long Beach
California School Library Association
California Library Association
American Library Association
And librarians everywhere

CONTENTS

PREFACE

When school librarians have so much to do—as do other members of the learning community—and have expanded their mission, and because students really need a network of community support, mutual partnerships are vital for effective learning at all ages. However, partnerships themselves require substantial investments of time and effort if they are expected to have a positive impact on learning. The goal is to identify and optimize potential collaborations in ways that foster library media programs and advance the learning community in general.

This volume is intended to help library media teachers understand the nature of partnerships, at both individual and group levels. It details the steps for developing and maintaining partnerships, particularly with groups. It also demonstrates how technology can affect these educational collaborative efforts.

Chapter 1 describes the learning community, the importance of information literacy for its constituents, and the role of the library media teacher within the larger context of the community at large.

Before developing partnerships, the library media teacher must assess the library media program itself. Chapter 2 explains how standards and principles of such programs help the library staff assess the present program and identify areas in which partnerships can improve the library media center. Chapter 3 then explains how the library media teacher can provide leadership within the learning community.

Chapter 4 addresses how technology has affected the learning community in general and collaborative efforts in particular. It discusses how technology has permeated social consciousness and points out its opportunities as well as its limitations in terms of community building.

With grounding in library media programs and technology, the library media teacher can then explore the nature of partnerships. Chapter 5 explains the nature of groups, both as a set of individuals and as a group identity. The chapter discusses how groups work together and change over time. Chapter 6 then details the process by which the library media teacher can identify potential partners and gain their support.

Chapters 7 through 13 cover different partnership stakeholders, identifying the niche and manner of operation of each, then providing samples of ways in which library media teachers can collaborate with those stakeholders in brief summaries and longer case studies. Chapter 7 deals with different constituents in schools: teachers, support staff, administrators, other library staff, school boards, and students. It also discusses effective means to communicate within the school setting. Chapter 8 covers family partnerships and focuses on volunteers in a technological age. Chapter 9 explores the inner workings of institutions of higher education and points out mutual professional development and research opportunities. Chapter 10 discusses traditional and vanguard partnerships with different types of libraries and shows how mutual advocacy can advance all library programs. Chapter 11 covers government and social community agencies. It also notes the role of mass media as a local tool for community building. Chapter 12 focuses on professional organizations, both in the library world as well as in other like-minded associations, and how they can contribute to the learning community beyond their memberships. Chapter 13 demonstrates how businesses work hand in hand with libraries to their mutual satisfaction.

Because partnerships exist at different depths for different reasons, Chapter 14 details different levels of collaboration, from a single project to community improvement. Chapter 15 concludes by describing ways to coordinate and optimize partnership impact. References and additional readings provide the reader with more ideas to use in partnerships to improve library media programs.

The process and product of partnerships both strengthen the leadership role of the library media teacher and provide effective ways in which to have an impact on library media programs and improve the learning community. The interdependency that exists through collaboration models the educational weave that supports present and future society.

The Web sites listed here were accessed in June 2001. The addresses were correct at that time, but the Internet is a volatile medium, and URLs often change or disappear altogether. If you find you are unable to find a URL listed here, try shortening it to just after the .edu, .org, or .com to locate the home page of the author or organization; it may be possible to locate the specific site using links from the main page.

THE LEARNING COMMUNITY

The phrase "it takes a village to raise a child" has become a cliché. Knock-off books discuss how it takes a city—or a world—to prepare our children. On the other hand, one also hears that it takes only one consistent, caring adult to keep a child on track. What is the reality?

In today's world it is all too easy to lose sight of an individual child. "It's the parent's responsibility." "The school needs to do its job." "The kid has to assume responsibility." "It's society's fault." As long as the burden is delegated to someone else, the other parties don't feel obligated to worry. The truth is, from the moment a child wakes up to the moment that child goes to sleep, someone needs to support, to guide, that child. In fact, at-risk students tend to be those young folks who slip through the daily cracks in a societal cry of "I thought he was with *you!*"

The burden of responsibility for children is too much to bear for any one person or institution. That's where community comes into play. In the traditional scenario, everyone knew everyone else—and their business. The norms were explicit, and the consequences of violating them predictable. The status quo, both in terms of staying within the locale and of following the family or local trade, ruled the day. Choices were fewer, and deviations from the usual choices were more noticeable. Those who didn't fit the mold either became outcast or assumed their own special identities within the community.

Now the choices are myriad, and most communities are much less stable. The numbers of people can be daunting, as are the tasks that need to be done. But kids still need to "get grown" and have some preparation to take on life's responsibilities. Schools are still seen as a community good, an agency for the upbringing of children. They are legislated by law and funded publicly (even if inadequately). As much as the citizenry lambastes education, it depends on it for its very future. The fear of school failure actually signals the extent to which people desperately cling to the hope that schools will take care of the young.

Schools have taken on more tasks than ever before. They teach values that once were the primary domain of organized religion. They teach sex education, which mom and dad were supposed to explain (or the community was supposed to protect their children from). They teach cooperation and manners, another family job. They offer before- and after-school activities. They even provide food and childcare. It's too much, especially without the support of the rest of the community.

So can there be a sense of community these days? Yes; in fact, the problem is that there are too many communities. The question is: What *is* a community? At its most basic, a community is a stable group of people with similar values and attitudes; a sense of community arises more out of faith than facts. Traditionally, a small town constituted a community, with well-defined roles, expectations, and norms. Communication was consistent and regular. Stability was ensured because families didn't move often, and children generally followed in their parents' footsteps. In today's world, the sense of community has changed parameters. In large urban areas, neighborhoods may proclaim themselves to be communities, sometimes focusing on a religious or social gathering place. In other cases, nuclear families may reach out to their extended families or find similar families with common backgrounds or values. Cyberspace provides another community; although some students may have less time with family members because of Internet activity, those same Netters may be developing other forms of community in a world that feels unwelcome to them. In any case, the need and search for community persists.

The Learning Community

The curriculum is changing, students are changing, formats for learning are changing, even society is changing. So it is no small wonder that teachers also need to change. The question is, how? Particularly with grades due the next day and insufficient time scheduled for staff development or collaboration, teachers may feel daunted by the need to learn "one more thing." What is all this pressure? With the burst of information and the complexities of society, all influenced by technology, today's students need to learn more—and learn how to learn, because they will probably hold jobs that have not been imagined yet.

Differentiated learning, increased use of individual educational plans (IEPs), incorporation of technology, articulation: All point to added work. Standards and outcomes-based learning increase the stakes in teacher work. Consider districts that are developing graduation outcomes. Tamalpais Union High School District (Larkspur, California) already requires evidence of student proficiency in three such outcomes, with eleven more being rolled out. Because portfolios are being used to provide authentic assessment, teachers and students feel overwhelmed by the possible data collection processes.

A culture of learning helps to mitigate individual burdens, because it helps to align efforts, thereby optimizing support for the entire community. Learning-centered cultures tend to display several of the psychological characteristics described by the Learner-Centered Principles Work Group of the American Psychological Association's Board of Educational Affairs (1997):

- They facilitate conscious construction of meaning from information and experience and link learning with existing knowledge.

- They foster goal setting for personal and academic learning.

- They build a repertoire of thinking and reasoning strategies, including metacognition.

- They advocate contextual learning and optimize the learning environment and educational practice.

- They emphasize intrinsic motivations to learn and also facilitate the learner's effort and commitment to learn.

- They provide developmentally appropriate learning opportunities.

- They enhance learning through social interactions.

- They attend to individual differences in learning and take into account the learner's background (socioeconomic, linguistic, cultural).

- They set high standards and assess all aspects of education regularly.

How Does Information Literacy Help Learning?

The concept of learning *how* to learn has become as important as *what* to learn. One of the sets of literacy competencies being touted these days is "information literacy," basically the ability to access, evaluate, and use information from a variety of sources. In the past, these competencies may have been called "library skills" and were taught by a librarian or by a teacher from an English grammar book. However, the definition of information literacy has expanded greatly to encompass numerous formats, the generation of information rather than merely the repetition of existing facts, and social aspects of literacy such as ethical use and collaboration. Underlying processes of data manipulation, reflective analysis of ideas, and dynamics of collaboration contribute to learning across the curriculum. Gone are the days of mindless rote learning.

The American Association of School Librarians and the Association for Educational Communications and Technology (1998) have developed nine information literacy standards for students. These competencies fall into three categories: *information literacy* (access, evaluation, and use of information), *independent learning* (pursuing information for personal interest, appreciating creative expression, seeking and generating knowledge), and *social responsibility* (information's importance in democracy, ethical behavior, collaboration). Certainly, students need to examine fact and opinion, analyze content, and synthesize prior knowledge throughout their academic lives. The issue is how those processes are taught and learned in meaningful ways.

Enter the library media teacher—in collaboration with classroom teachers. Library media teachers bring cross-curricular knowledge and technological expertise to the table along with their traditional bibliographic skill. It is obvious that teachers cannot assume, "It's Tuesday, so it must be *Reader's Guide to Literature* day." Out of context, learning how to locate a magazine, or even how to evaluate a Web site, has little significance for students. Instead, library media teachers understand the intellectual underpinnings of information literacy and can work with classroom teachers to further content learning through the incorporation of these procedural competencies. Thus, if students are debating a current issue for a civics class, they quickly understand that magazines would be good sources for different perspectives on specific topics. Students then realize the importance of finding relevant articles efficiently, and they quickly pick up the skill of using magazine indexes and abstracts. By planning a learning activity in the library in collaboration with the library media teacher, the classroom teacher facilitates the students' gathering and shaping of facts.

Such project-based, information-processing learning develops higher level thinking and is more stimulating for teachers and students alike. Who wants to grade the same answer twenty or forty times? Students have more investment in topics that they choose and can manipulate creatively. Because different topics can be explored, students can learn from each other's efforts along with their own work. Sharing their new knowledge, students can learn more deeply *and* broadly so teachers can, in effect, "cover" more content.

At times, the complexity of information literacy can be overwhelming. Schoolwide collaboration is necessary to facilitate effective gain and transference of literacy skills. By working collaboratively and incorporating information literacy, classroom and library media teachers can foster lifelong learning in meaningful contexts, in an educationally refreshing manner. Rather than feeling more burdened, classroom teachers can share their work with librarians and expand their own repertoires of instructional strategies.

Case Study

At Redwood High School, teachers bemoaned the lack of student ability to critically evaluate sources, document their work, and use a variety of research strategies. As the library media teacher, I had developed a scope-and-sequence for "library skills" several years earlier, but teachers did not take it to heart. This time, another teacher and I co-chaired an action research plan effort to determine the desired student outcomes for information literacy, identify when and where those skills were being taught or applied, and provide means for teachers and students to work on those skills.

A literature review uncovered national and state information literacy standards and rubrics. The research committee (composed of department representatives as well as the co-chairs) synthesized the findings and developed a research skills instruction "inventory." All departments reviewed the list and its wording. Then they examined their own practice in light of the inventory, identifying those skills that they taught or asked students to use and at which grade level. Complementing this task, the co-chairs conducted content analyses on research project assignments. Student focus groups provided another perspective on information literacy instruction and learning.

As a whole, the faculty agreed on the grade level and departmental responsibility for teaching research skills. Agreement also entailed ensuring that each course section, no matter who taught it, would include the specified information literacy instruction; American history, for example, would always include an assignment incorporating primary source research. Knowing that other teachers would deal with a specific information skill enabled teachers in upper grades to build on the students' prior knowledge.

Some interventions across the curriculum came to light as a result. Standardized bibliographic style sheets (for the Modern Language Association and American Psychological Association styles) were developed and used throughout high school. An outdated research handbook was updated and enhanced so students could use sections as guidesheets for focused efforts on one aspect of the research strategy process. The handbook was given to all faculty, too, and the contents were placed on the library's Web page for instant access at school or from home.

Two nagging issues for most teachers were plagiarism and Internet use. Study revealed that students were more apt to copy when they could not access or evaluate sources well. Therefore, the required computer literacy course added a unit on navigating and evaluating the Internet, which I first taught and then showed teachers how to use to guide students. Additionally, the research committee developed two Internet in-services for all faculty, one on plagiarism and the use of the Internet as a means for students to use "cheat" sites to download papers and another on positive ways that the Internet could help teachers develop creative plagiarism-proof lessons. Teachers became much more aware of the benefits and pitfalls of the Internet, and they discovered how to revitalize their own instruction and assignments to engage students more creatively. As an outreach effort, I also trained parents in how to use the Internet with their children. Not only did this workshop reinforce school practices, it helped parents understand controversial Internet issues and realize that they should get involved in their children's education.

The Moral Is . . .

Some of the results of incorporating information literacy into teaching follow:

More articulate and creative assignments

Greater emphasis on the entire research process

Closer examination of classroom practice and willingness to change as needed

Improved and expanded use of the Internet by faculty and students

More faculty interaction and curriculum-centered discussion

Greater alignment between professional development and classroom practice

Greater curricular coordination among teachers

More preplanning between classroom teachers and the library media teacher

Increased student engagement and achievement

Other schools have heard about this action research and have done their own in-service training based on this model. Redwood's feeder schools, in particular, have used parts of the project to inform their own practice as well as improve articulation between middle and high school.

Overarching issues, such as information literacy, can rally library media and classroom teachers to improve their practice and facilitate mutual professional development and coordination. Everyone wins—especially the students.

Library Media Teachers and the Larger Community

The collaborative effort described previously demonstrates just one facet of the learning community as a whole. In that situation, the following contributions were made and benefits realized:

- The library media teacher spearheaded the study and acted as a catalyst to get information literacy integrated throughout the curriculum.

- Teachers examined their own and others' curriculum areas and were trained to share responsibility for helping their students become information literate.

- Administrators provided support and received funding, as well as seeing student scores increase.

- Parents learned about the Internet and became more involved in their children's education.

- Feeder school librarians calibrated their information literacy programs and served as a model for other feeder schools to improve their own library programs and staffing.

- The regional foundation underwrote the project and facilitated the dissemination of this action research model to other sites.

- Professional library organizations provided information literacy standards and rubrics and received information about the action research to help advance the profession.

Although reform-based funding propelled this action research project, collaborative efforts in general can occur daily. They can involve all types of partners within the school and in the community: civic and social groups, organizations, libraries, other educational institutions, businesses, and government. The main impetus remains student improvement, the main catalyst the willingness to work together, and the main process reflective action.

Librarians can play a significant role in each type of educational partnership because of their unique skills and contacts:

Daily interaction with the entire school community

Knowledge of all curricular areas and associated resources

Professional contacts with other types of librarians and associated professional organizations

Community membership (e.g., parent, voter, taxpayer, participant in religious/social activity)

Information and research knowledge

Organizational and access skills

Administrative and collaborative skills

Technological skills

Communication skills

Librarians cannot perform their professional duties without collaboration. As collaborators, they provide a realistic model for others to adopt and adapt.

LIBRARY MEDIA PROGRAMS

For library media teachers to participate substantively in collaborative projects, they must know and manage their own turf first. As they model effective library programs and communicate their work to the learning community, they attract others and lay the foundation for successful improvement of their own programs as well as other's work. School reform efforts testify to the need for collaboration throughout the community to provide young people with the skills needed to be prepared for life. In today's technological world, the library can offer access to information worldwide as well as a repertoire of tools for grappling with this information effectively.

In 1998 the American Association of School Librarians (AASL) and the Association for Educational and Communications Technology (AECT) produced *Information Power: Guidelines for Effective Library Media Programs*. The guidelines assert that the mission of the library media program is "to ensure that students and staff are effective users of ideas and information," which is made possible partly by working with other educators. In fact, the guidelines point to "the development of a community of learners that is centered on the student and sustained by a creative, energetic library media program" (AASL & AECT, 1998, p. 6). This document provides the theoretical grounding for working collaboratively to ensure lifelong learning.

Standards

As do other school programs, the library media program includes standards for students. In the library's domain, these are categorized as information literacy standards. The library media teacher must collaborate with the school community to make sure that these standards are met. When teachers read and understand these standards in light of their own practice and content standards, they consider themselves to be the main facilitators of information literacy instruction (Farmer, 2000a).

As stated in Chapter 1, the nine information literacy standards identified by AASL and AECT are divided into three categories: information literacy, independent learning, and social responsibility. Within each category three standards describe desired behaviors and competencies. Partnership opportunities abound across the standards, many of which incorporate technology:

1. *Access information effectively.* Classes e-mail students in remote countries about global issues. Students interview senior citizens about local history. Naturalists teach students how to use science probes to test community water.

2. *Evaluate information competently.* The library media teacher and classroom teacher team teach how to evaluate Web sites. Health professionals help students develop individualized fitness plans based on fitness tests and body measurements. With local campaign organizers, students analyze political advertisements.

3. *Use information accurately and creatively.* Students write letters to legislators about social issues, develop business plans, and create field guides to local flora.

4. *Pursue information related to personal interests.* Students comparison shop online, develop monthly budgets based on local information, and create databases of local teen volunteer opportunities.

5. *Appreciate literature and other creative expressions.* Students visit radio stations and help civic theater companies. Authors speak at school and are videotaped for later viewing and broadcasting.

6. *Strive for excellence in information seeking and knowledge generation.* Students create electronic portfolios, conduct "slam" poetry events, and participate in mock United Nations sessions.

7. *Recognize the importance of information to a democratic society.* Students compare newspaper coverage in different countries, participate in voting campaigns, and interview foreign exchange students.

8. *Practice ethical behavior in regard to information and information technology.* Students present PowerPoint talks to younger classes about computer ethics, write ethics policies, and cite research sources on their Web pages.

9. *Participate effectively in groups to pursue and generate information.* Students partner online to create multimedia presentations on scientific concepts, create skits on immigration experiences using interview information, and create Web pages for nonprofit agencies.

In each of the activities mentioned, young people are interacting with others under the planned structure of partnerships, whether within the school or in the community or linked to the world. The goal is student achievement, and the means is collaborative instruction and the development of an inquiry-based learning environment.

Library Media Program Principles

Studies done in Colorado in 1994 and 1998 and replicated in Alaska and Pennsylvania (Lance, Rodney & Hamilton-Pennell, 2000) found the greatest single educational factor in student achievement to be high-quality library programs.

This brings up the questions: What constitutes high quality, and how can library media programs improve? How can library media teachers carry out their mission to ensure that students and staff are effective users of ideas?

We can answer these questions by using the twenty-seven principles researched and codified by AASL and AECT (1998), the cardinal premises on which effective school library media programs are based. Like the information literacy standards for students, these principles are divided into three categories: learning and teaching, information access and delivery, and program administration.

Within that framework, a main tenet for school library media teachers to carry out their mission is the need to build strong educational partnerships. The question is: Which partnerships are the most effective relative to each guiding principle? Because library staff are usually working at full capacity, they need to optimize their partnership opportunities. If, for example, the entire school community thinks that Principle 2 ("information literacy standards . . . are integral to . . . the curriculum") is most likely to be realized through classroom teacher efforts, the library media teacher should partner closely with that group.

To that end, I designed and administered a survey to K–12 school community members (a sample of administrators, classroom teachers, library staff, and students) in Long Beach and Orange County (California). The survey listed each information literacy principle, and respondents indicated its relative potential importance on five-point Likert scales. Respondents also indicated the key decision maker for each principle.

The main conclusion I drew from the survey was that the school community *does* pay attention to the library media program, and values it. They expect good collections and management and will support library funding to that end, providing information is the core. In fact, homogeneity of perception existed *across constituents* about the value of individual library principles. Such attitudes should enable library media teachers to pursue what they think are priorities in library media programs and to spend their time partnering with perceived key decision makers. In terms of advancing information literacy and inquiry-based learning, library media teachers would do well to facilitate teacher power because teachers think they control that arena; independent action by library media teachers may backfire. The locus of control on administrative issues is seen as a function of local decision making.

On the other hand, the survey showed wide variance—especially among teachers—in the relative importance placed on the principles. Library media teachers might try a more systematic approach to educating that group. Because many think staff development is in the administrators' hands, if library media teachers can influence that activity and gain recognition and power in this area, they may change teachers' opinions about library media programs.

In general, library media teachers would do well to focus on efforts considered to be high priority for the school community. Providing and managing resources (including access) that are integrated into the curriculum remain the core values across constituencies. Instructional issues were not considered to be as critical, so if library media teachers believe in their significance within that role, they must either educate the school community about their expertise—and the importance of instruction in general—or not spend so much time on that endeavor. It should also be noted that intellectual freedom and community links were uniformly *not* considered important; it appears that constituents were more interested in fulfilling their own immediate agendas.

The implication is clear that library media teachers must work in concert with school constituents to improve the library media program. Planning behind the scenes has been the usual approach; it is time for library media teachers to make those partnerships more visible to students and other community members to emphasize the need for collaboration. Of course, results will vary from site to site. Library media teachers might consider conducting a similar survey for their own sites to help them educate their constituents about the library media program and prioritize their own collaborative efforts.

Setting the Stage for Partnerships

As library media teachers begin to think about partnerships, their own vision of library media programs should be clear. Because school libraries exist within the school culture, library media teachers should explore its historical context; this investigation will help contextualize statements such as, "We've always done it like this." Library media teachers new to a school should consult a savvy long-termer to get the lay of the land before making substantial changes or pursuing certain partners. It isn't necessary for library media teachers to go along with past practice, but they need to know the library's history so they will have a better idea of how change will probably be accepted—and can determine what assumptions community members might bring to the table. From there, library media teachers can assess the program's current status as well as the learning community's situation. Only then can goals and objectives be determined realistically and in alignment with the school's mission.

Once library media teachers have a clear picture of their library media programs, they are poised to communicate about it with potential partners. A good start is to answer the following questions about the program to "sell" it convincingly:

- Why does the school library exist?

- What are its historical roots within the democracy and within the specific community?

- What are the program's important qualities and values?

- What are the program's distinctive features?

- Whom does the library serve?

- What key words have special meaning for the library?

Close Up

Teaching and Learning

This online activity can be used with teachers or students to examine ways to conduct research.

Research Processes

Compare at least two of the research tutorial sites listed below. Discuss how you might use/adapt/be inspired by them in your classroom in collaboration with the library media teacher.

http://Multiweb.lib.calpoly.edu/infocomp/modules/index.html

http://library.jmu.edu/library/gold/modules.htm

http://www.wsulibs.wsu.edu/usered/aml/activities/acthome.html

http://www.infopeople.org/howto
A state-funded series (also look at IWWW and AdvSearch)

http://www.researchpaper.com
Advice about researching papers online, etc.

Information Access and Delivery

This is an online activity for students and teachers. It emphasizes access to reference resources and emphasizes the need for critical analysis.

Reference Resources

Introduction

Online reference service can consist of several options: specific reference sites (such as www.fedstats.gov, which provides federal statistics), megasites (basically, bibliographies of bibliographies), information literacy (at least Internet) tutorials, other types of guide pages on how to do research, tips on evaluating Web sites, lists of assignments, online help, and reading motivation (book chats, book lists, online contests, etc.).

In this session, you will be examining some of these options and using sites to evaluate and compare sources. You may want to bookmark some of these addresses for future use. You should also bring a disk to each class session.

Activity

1. Using at least two of the evaluation guidelines/rubrics listed below, compare at least two of the listed reference megasites.

2. Within each megasite, compare at least two related reference resources.

- Evaluation Web sites for reference services:

    - http://discoveryschool.com/schrockguide

    - http://www.personal.psu.edu/users/w/x/wxh139/e valu/topic.htm

    - http://wlma.org/libint/evalweb.html

    - http://lib.nmsu.edu/instruction/eval.html

    - http://milton.mse.jhu.edu:8001/research/education/net.html

- Megasites:

    - http://www.lausd.k12.ca.us/lausd/offices/instruct/itb/ libserv/dl.htm#ss

    - www.libertynet.org/lion/ready.html

    - www.ala.org/parents/index.html

    - www.ala.org/publicpage/index.html

    - www.digital-librarian.com

    - www.refdesk.com

    - www.ipl.org

    - dir.yahoo.com/reference/index.html

    - libraries.ucsd.edu/refshelf.html

    - www.inform.umd.edu/EdRes/Topic

    - mel.lib.mi.us

    - www.cc.columbia.edu/cu/lweb/eguides

Program Administration

This online activity is geared toward library media teachers but may be adapted for other technology planners. It provides some starting points and emphasizes human dynamics in technology planning.

Grant Guidance for Technology

Grantsmanship has become a staple of library media teacher life. As you envision the library media program, jot down a couple of technology-related projects that require outside funding.

1. Go to LibraryLand at http://www.sunsite.berkeley.edu/LibraryLand/ admin/bud.htm. Read over some of the resources, then note some of the grantsmanship tips you found that might apply to your effort.

2. The culture in which you function and the partnerships you form help shape the kind of technology grants that will be supported and implemented. Go to Applied Systems Analysis and Processing at http://www.appliedsys.net/tvp-overview.htm. Analyze the different charts to explore the issues of change and impact.

3. Based on the information you have collected, sketch out how you might develop a technology plan. Some guiding Web sites are listed below:

    http://compaq.edmin.com

    http://nsba.org/sbot/toolkit/index.html

    http://archives.ncsa.uiuc.edu/IDT/html/Planning/
    planning_process.html

    Digital High School (look under http://www.ctap.k12.ca.us)

LEADING FROM THE MIDDLE

3

Is the library truly the hub of the school? Consider: If all the curricular and co-curricular efforts go out from that hub, then the library itself is not moving much—except, hopefully, forward. Perhaps a better image is that of mountain climbing, where each person helps the other attain the final goal. There is a difference, however, that must be acknowledged: Theoretically, the library media teacher works with every entity in the school community, every child and every adult and in all curricular areas. In that respect, using the mountain climbing analogy, the library media teacher seems more like the photographer of the climb, except that library media teachers provide lifelines.

Another difference in this scenario is that library media teachers do not always know what the mountain really looks like or the best path to take. They have to remember the other mountains they have climbed to develop a best-case strategy. Ideally, library media teachers can choose the mountain, the goal. But before they can even begin that task, they have to know themselves and their mission. The beginning hiker doesn't choose Mt. Everest as the first climb; one must know one's limits. The climber must also determine the reason for the job ahead. What is the library media center's mission? That decision is not an individual one for the library media teacher. Although the library media teacher is the key person and can influence the media center's mission, the center's charge is constrained by the school's mission and must be aligned to it. That mission must be crystal clear to the library media teacher and the rest of the school community.

Defining the Other

Determining the media center's mission requires a background check of the school. What are the aims of the school? Both explicit and implicit agendas must be acknowledged. Obviously, the easiest way to begin is to analyze "official" documents: annual reports or "report cards," handbooks for each community constituent (student, staff, parent, community at large), newsletters, Web pages, meeting minutes, budget figures, and student publications. The community at large also produces documents about the school: news articles, broadcasts, and mentions in chambers of commerce and real estate brochures. This first check can also uncover possible inconsistencies in image: If the school says it's wonderful and the locals overlook or underestimate the school's worth, then major public relations work needs to be done to align these perceptions.

As with other evaluations, different methods must be used to triangulate the findings. Direct observation and verbal interaction come into play. The principal is the obvious person to interview because that person is ostensibly the chief decision maker. (If the principal is not the one in charge, that information should be discovered early on.) What does that chief officer think about the school? What does that person value? How is that value translated into action and resource allocation? While the library media teacher has that captive audience, he or she should find out how the principal relates to the library media center. What does he or she consider the library's role and mission to be? What role does the library media teacher play? Of course, a formal interview should be balanced with real activity-based interaction such as joint committee work and schoolwide initiatives.

To get a sense of other key school community members, the library media teacher should see them in their natural environment and work with them at least in neutral terms if not entirely on their own turf. From these interactions the library media teacher can find out how consistently and cohesively a school operates. When consistency and cohesion are high, the media center's mission is easier to define. Where such organic integrity is not found, the library media teacher has a harder time maneuvering around the unknown factions but can take advantage of having more freedom to define the media center's mission. Although a positive, cohesive school environment may seem optimum, that same atmosphere can make it harder to improve or to try new angles. No scenario is perfect; the library media teacher must scope out the scene and respond in a way to make the media center the most effective part of the community.

Leveraging the Library

Even the most experienced climber needs to know what resources are available before setting a climbing goal. Likewise, the library media teacher must determine what resources are available for short-term and long-term goals. The mission may be clear, but the means to achieve that mission are defined by resources.

If the overarching goal is to develop a learning community, then the library media teacher must look to both the media center's resources and external resources. Starting with the center itself, the library media teacher must determine how the center can make a unique contribution. What niche can it fill? Having defined the mission of the school and couched the mission of the library within those parameters, the library media teacher can build upon existing—or potential—strengths.

Information storage and retrieval is an important strength. The media center has the greatest access to information in the school community. But perhaps as important as the "stuff" itself is the library media teacher's ability to research, to ferret out details from the wealth of information and misinformation. The savvy library media teacher has a repertoire of search strategies unequaled by other school communities. Where was that report on the benefits of technology to increase reading achievement? What do experts say is the best way to involve parents in school decisions? What are the pros and cons of year-round schooling? These are the types of school reform questions that library media teachers can answer quickly so chief decision makers can proceed on their own.

The library media center is also known for being *organized.* What details must be addressed in a particular plan? How can all the constituents keep in contact? How can information be distributed? If there are a number of different task forces, how can those minutes and tasks be kept in order? What about evidence to further a reform plan? The library media teacher can organize the documents and the expertise in a variety of ways to match the objectives.

As mentioned before, the library media teacher has the advantage of *working with all constituents.* He or she can more easily see the overlapping efforts of each body. This makes for more effective coordination and assessment. Although the administration oversees all the school efforts, the library media teacher is in the direct line of fire of possibly conflicting priorities. Library media teachers provide higher-ups with a credible reality check.

Media centers and library media teachers are also in the vanguard of *accessible resources,* with the center being open long hours daily (hopefully) in a neutral area. Library media centers are, in fact, becoming the natural town hall setting where the "war" of ideas can be discussed safely. A safe and open environment, in terms of space as well as atmosphere, is a real advantage of media centers and certainly makes them natural negotiating locations. Additionally, with school library media centers increasingly creating Web sites, those virtual interactive environments offer 24/7 community space for action. Space is intellectual as much as it is physical.

Just to muddy the waters a bit, the library media center may play different roles with different groups—in a sense becoming a chameleon according to the needs of specific groups: the researcher for administration, the negotiator for curriculum developers, the mentor for teachers, the coach for students, the catalyst for technology specialists, the safety net for counselors, the advisor for parents. Likewise, the approach that the library media teacher takes with these different groups may vary according to the task at hand, the type of personalities involved, the number of people participating, the time frame, and so forth. One could become schizophrenic or at least conflicted in these different roles, so the need for a clear mission or purpose and a realistic sense of resources is of paramount importance. If done effectively, flexible "loose coupling" or coordination of apparently differing efforts can actually enrich the total library program. One key to success is that same creative organization for which the library media teacher is known.

Library Media Teacher as Change Agent

It should be mentioned that the library media center's mission and role might change over time as the school community changes. The resources must reflect current supply and demand, which is often a moving target. In the context of school reform, the media center must be able to realign efforts. The more global the perspective, the more stable the mission or role. School library media centers have as a long-term goal to provide resources that support the curriculum. Where the mission changes is in the types of resources available and their use. Likewise, although a basic tenet is to provide access to information, over time (and depending on several other factors), the concept of storage has become less important. Library media teachers have seen this change in the past in the form of resource sharing and photocopying, and now they see the Internet and possible other access points as shifting paradigms for resource development and maintenance.

In terms of the instructional role, the library media teacher has moved from direct-and-point to click-and-point—and process. Instruction now entails working with a broader spectrum of the school community and the community at large. Moreover, instruction comes in more "flavors": signage, self-guided tours, Web tutorials, videotape presentations, and interactive simulations. Quite a potpourri from which to choose!

Library media teachers should embrace change because, at its heart, learning is changed behavior. Change is inevitable, so it makes sense for library media teachers to face changing issues and deal with them effectively, thus influencing the future at least to some degree. Certainly, planned change is easier to accommodate than unplanned change. But if library media teachers choose not to deal with change, outside forces will make the decisions affecting library media programs. Following are some pointers to help library media teachers create positive change for the library program:

- Observe changing trends in the community: demographics, values, behaviors, pressures. Consider how these changes might affect the library and create a vision for the library. Look especially at areas lacking equilibrium; they are most vulnerable to change.

- Work from a strong, safe foundation. Then if regrouping is necessary, there is something solid to fall back on.

- Share knowledge and resources. Be available and receptive. Be visible. Give timely and useful feedback. People will appreciate the openness and will be more willing to network in return.

- Be a lifelong learner. Seek professional and program improvement.

Library media teachers can make the loop, be in the loop, be out of the loop, or think there is no loop. In their reputed role within the school, they are best poised as leading partners in the loop of change.

Close Up

This series of workshops was designed by a network of school library media teachers who wanted to have an impact on library service throughout the county by training teachers in literacy activities. The announcement for this series of workshops is included here.

Continuing Education Workshop Series

Literature: Live!

A series of two-hour workshops conducted by the Marin School Librarians in conjunction with the Marin County Office of Education.

These workshops will be held from 4:00 P.M. to 6:00 P.M. at the MCOE the first Monday of each month, beginning in October, for nine months. Each workshop will feature top literature, include demonstrations of ways to foster reading literacy and enjoyment. Participants will receive practical tips and handouts at each session, and will be able to share ideas and concerns. Dinner treats are included in the registration fee ($15 for IMC members; $20 for non-members). Teachers may attend any or all of the series; it is hoped that ongoing participation will engender a strong group spirit and a viable support team (minimum number of attendees per session: 10; maximum of 50).

The workshops will comprise three trimester strands: booktalking, integrating literature into the curriculum, and resource-based learning incorporating technology. In addition, each session will focus on a particular age group. Hopefully, teachers will pick up valuable ideas from every session.

Booktalking: Oct.–Dec.; Integration: Jan.–Mar.; Resources: Apr.–June

Primary: Oct., Jan., Apr.; Upper elementary: Nov., Feb., May, Jr./Sr. High: Dec., Mar., June

Oct. 7: *Introducing Booktalking: Picture Books and Easy Readers*

Enjoy sparking the interest of the youngest student by sharing high quality picture books and first readers. Listen to professional librarians tell about classics and current greats! Learn different booktalk techniques, including the use of props and aids. Get tips on how to make students not only reading-ready but reading-hungry!

Nov. 4: *Introducing Booktalking for Upper Elementary Grades*

Guide 3rd through 6th graders to engaging literature through booktalks and other book sharing techniques. Watch how the professionals—librarians—do it. A variety of reading material will be shared: poetry, plays, myths and legends, and even riddles!

Dec. 2: *Introducing Literature with Pre-Teens*

Get even the "coolest" twelve year old and up to embrace literature with these proven techniques in booktalking and literature-sharing. Learn about reader's advising, reading theater, book discussion groups, and student storytelling. Help students grow up with great words and ideas.

Jan. 6: *Weaving Literature into Primary Grade Activities*

What's one of the best ways to experience something? Read about it! Whether it's sitting behind the pilot's cockpit, feeling the pains of moving, or wondering, "Why, indeed, did the mosquito get its buzz?", literature connects with both mind and heart. Hear about books and fun follow-up activities that involve children and help them internalize great literature.

Feb. 3: *Incorporating Literature into Upper Elementary Units*

It's one thing to memorize a date or draw a map: it's another to feel like the first Native American girl to see European ships! That's the magic of literature! Get great ideas on how to link great books and other literature to classroom studies. Share enrichment activities that will help students reach the next plateau in reading literacy—and pleasure.

Mar. 3: *Enriching Jr./Sr. High School Curriculum through Literature*

Take advantage of those adolescent hormones and needs for self-identity by including literature into the curriculum. Find new ways for students to experience the plight—and fight—of medieval girls; help boys feel what it means to be different—and conquer! In short, learn how to make academia come alive through literature.

Apr. 7: *Resource-Based Learning for Primary Grades*

You already know that young students learn by doing. Expand your repertoire of learning tools by sharing ideas for thematic projects that take advantage of your school library's resources. Learn some new ways to bridge thematic units and literature and incorporate technology into the process.

May 5: *Resource-Based Learning for Upper Elementary Grades*

As schools try to teach the WHOLE child, they encourage projects that transcend textbooks and meet the individual and group needs of children. Learn creative and time-effective ways to use a variety of resources, including electronic, to reach the wide variety of students in your classes.

June 2: *Resource-Based Learning for Jr./Sr. High School*

Key terms these days? Meaningful learning, critical thinking skills, authentic assessment. These goals can be met effectively through resource-based projects. See how librarians and teachers together can design thoughtful and engaging learning experiences using a wide range of resources and incorporating technology.

TECHNOLOGY AS A MEANS AND AN END

Technology is pervasive in society, and hopefully in the learning community and the library media center in particular. Be it electronic library catalogs, Internet connections, or even a telephone line, technology can facilitate the access to, use of, and communication of information. Library media centers should use these technological tools collaboratively as a means and an end relative to their programs.

What Is Special about Technology?

How technology affects the learning community depends on the choice and deployment of the technology. In a worst-case scenario, technology impeded education because the computers and their boxes were left in the halls, and people had to step around them to get to class or meetings. In a best-case scenario, the infusion of technology fostered equitable education by drawing communities together, helping students access and use information in rich variety and expanding the school's impact in the community. Using technology to replicate old practices—such as using a computer to make library date due cards—does not take advantage of its unique features. Rather, new ways demand new perspectives and new services that would not have been possible before, such as electronically generated collection maps. Some of the critical features of technology are the collapse of time and space, the combination of different media, sophisticated processing, and the ability to repurpose information easily.

Collapse of Time and Space

Meetings can be held at any time and in any place where networking can connect people, be it via the Internet or telephone. People do not even need to meet at the same time to collaborate. One can say that traditional mail accomplishes this same task, but it does so much more slowly. In addition, documents transmitted via telecommunication lines can be modified in real time by several

23

people simultaneously using NetMeeting or even word processing "tracing" features. This latter technology, available in current versions of Word, color codes changes and allows the commenter to insert electronic "post-its" to expand on the markings.

Threaded discussion is another communications improvement that owes a debt to technology. Using newsgroups, e-mail, or discussion "boards," participants can respond to individual comments while seeing the nonlinear development of the total conversation. Sometimes a topic veers off in one direction and results in a better solution than if a strict sequence were maintained. Additionally, the ideas are archived to ensure that thoughtful analyses can be followed up on.

Real time "chats" (Internet relay communication) offer people an inexpensive way to discuss topics without meeting face to face. More sophisticated programs, such as http://www.TappedIn.org, allow participants to show documents and Web sites during the discussion. Consider how useful this tool can be for IEP meetings with parents and educators, particularly when parents have difficulties getting away from their workplaces. These mandated sessions can be scheduled more easily, thus advancing interventions in a more timely way so students can benefit more quickly. As with threaded discussion, these sessions can be archived for proper IEP documentation history.

Combination of Media

Research into and experience with issues of multiple intelligences and learning styles affirm the usefulness of employing a variety of media when teaching and learning. Ideas do not live in an abstract vacuum; they have contextual meaning. Text also benefits from visual and aural cues. Pictures without captions can have ambiguous meanings. Isolated sounds may make no sense. The more these different media reinforce an idea, the stronger will be the impact of that idea. Technology facilitates this holistic approach to thinking and communicating.

CD-ROMs and DVDs and authoring and presentation software are the most obvious examples of this feature. CDs and DVDs are compact storage devices that can handle a variety of digital files. When students use an electronic encyclopedia, they can hear a national anthem, see how the rain cycle works, watch a historical event, analyze statistical tables and charts, and read significant facts. Although some people may think that the Internet will make these storage devices obsolete, technological advances have made individual production and recording onto CD-R/W discs financially reasonable. For less than 50 cents, students can store their entire high school electronic portfolio of work, including an electronic index to help the user access the specific document needed. Likewise, a library media center can create a compendium of information literacy learning aids and distribute them cheaply on CD so students with low-end computers without Internet access can acquire those skills. On a schoolwide or local level, a CD can feature several services in detail to help the community take advantage of useful expertise. In fact, with new video game systems having the ability to read CD-ROMs, many more families will be able to take advantage of CD-based information.

Authoring and presentation tools offer a rich learning and production environment. These software programs permit users to import or access text, graphics, sound, video, and Web pages in an almost seamless manner. Users can also vary the order of the "slides" to reflect their own thinking patterns and facilitate viewer control of the information. For example, a branching structured "stack" enables the viewer to choose those elements that are important or that need review. When authoring programs are used as learning aids, students can easily self-pace and self-direct their learning. Moreover, because individual stacks can be merged easily, partners can work collaboratively to develop sophisticated presentations that would take too long using more traditional methods.

Sophisticated Processing

Computers and other mechanized devices were created to facilitate repetitive or arduous calculations and processing. "Programmed" cards sped up weaving patterns. Babbage's calculating machine generated answers more quickly. Turing's machines analyzed codes more efficiently. Computers were originally regarded as "number crunchers." Thanks to high-powered computers, space missions can be dynamically redirected to ensure success. On a more immediate level, students use graphing calculators to generate graphical representations of complex functions quickly rather than by laboriously plotting lines dot by dot. With computers, students can now produce animations of scientific processes in a reasonable time. Library media teachers can generate a variety of usage reports using automated circulation programs. Students and educators can use spreadsheets to predict outcomes and can quickly see how changing factors may influence those possible outcomes. Schools must demonstrate accountability and use data to improve education, and sophisticated statistical packages enable administrators to disaggregate data in different ways to determine what patterns occur, thus determining which interventions would be most effective. In each case, the machines do the tedious processing, freeing people to concentrate on analysis.

Repurposing

With the increasing interoperability of digitized data, users can take existing documents and use them for new purposes. A library or school plan forms the basis of a grant proposal. Catalog entries can generate bibliographies. Digitized photos for the school newspaper can be imported for Open House presentations or school Web pages. Videotapes of individual or class work can be collected as a running portfolio of student performance assessment and progress. Data from a variety of sources, particularly useful when working with partners, can be collated and organized to form a cohesive and in-depth product.

Technology as an End

The combined features of technology lend themselves well to today's economic world. It is little wonder that government studies such as the Secretary's Commission on Achieving Necessary Skills, *What Work Requires of Schools* (1991) and the *Forum on the Future of Technology in Education* (2000) mention the need to produce technologically literate students ready for tomorrow's e-commerce world. One of the main reasons that the notion of the Digital Divide is so important is that inequities in access and use of technology result in economic barriers for underserved—and therefore unprepared—students. Realizing the impact of technology on the economy and education, the U.S. Department of Education reviewed its technology plan for the twenty-first century (2000a) and pledged to meet the following new goals:

- All students and teachers will have access to information technology in their classrooms, schools, communities, and homes.

- All teachers will use technology effectively to help students achieve high academic standards.

- All students will have technology and information literacy skills.

- Research and evaluation will improve the next generation of technology applications for teaching and learning.

- Digital content and networked applications will transform teaching and learning.

When looking at how children learn, technology has been shown to help students achieve, even without considering later economic incentives. First, *students must be aware* to learn; the neurons must be stimulated. Students respond to the novelty of technology and their ability to control it. These factors also address the emotional and motivational needs of students. Second, *students learn with their entire bodies*, so those activities that draw on different senses are more likely to engage them. Technology, with its combination of text, sound, image, and motion—along with the kinesthetic factors of working with the associated equipment—certainly reinforces different modes of learning. Third, *learning is largely a social endeavor*. Technology lends itself well to this process, be it working collaboratively to develop a multimedia presentation or a video production or telecommunicating with another person about an issue. Fourth, *learning is more effective if content embedded*, linked with ordinary experience. Technology facilitates the use of simulations and other problem-solving scenarios, which call on higher levels of critical thinking. Fifth, *each student learns uniquely*. To a large extent, students can control the pace and the scope of technology-enhanced learning. Technology can provide an open-ended learning environment in which students can explore ideas in structured ways. With diagnostic and management modes, computer-assisted learning software offers individualized instruction in most academic areas. In the final analysis, technology expands the repertoire of learning tools and offers an environment of exploration and immediate feedback.

It stands to reason that students must become technologically literate to take advantage of what technology can offer. With funding from the U.S. Department of Education, the International Society for Technology in Education (ISTE, 2000, p. 1) developed a series of technology standards for teachers. Their contention is that to live, learn, and work successfully in an increasingly complex and information-rich society, students and teachers must use technology effectively. Within a sound educational setting, technology can enable students to become:

- capable information technology users
- information seekers, analyzers, and evaluators
- problem solvers and decision makers
- creative and effective users of productivity tools
- communicators, collaborators, publishers, and producers
- informed, responsible, and contributing citizens.

In collaboration with twelve educational organizations and with co-sponsorship from government and business groups, ISTE (2000) categorized student technological skills and knowledge into six broad areas, with benchmark indicators at grades 2, 5, 8, and 12:

1. Basic operations and concepts
2. Social, ethical, and human issues
3. Technology productivity tools
4. Technology communication tools
5. Technology research tools
6. Technology problem-solving and decision-making tools.

For potential and practicing teachers, the categories were slightly modified. The following benchmark indicators were developed for general preparation, professional preparation, student teaching, and first-year teaching (ISTE, 2000):

Technology operations and concepts

Planning and designing learning environments and experiences

Teaching, learning, and the curriculum

Assessment and evaluation

Productivity and professional practice

Social, ethical, legal, and human issues

However fine the goal, sufficient support must be in place to ensure that all students and teachers can meet those goals. ISTE (2000) developed a set of essential conditions for implementing these standards, including

- a shared vision: systemic proactive leadership and administrative support;
- access to current technologies, software, and telecommunications networks;
- educators skilled in the use of technology for learning;

- professional development: consistent access to professional development to support technology use in teaching and learning;

- technical assistance for maintaining and using the technology;

- content standards and curriculum resources: educators knowledgeable in their content area, its standards, and its teaching methodologies;

- student-centered teaching;

- assessment: continuous evaluation of the effectiveness of technology for learning;

- community support to provide expertise, support, and resources; and

- support policies: structures for policies, finances, and rewards to support technology in learning.

As the school community focuses on student achievement, it must also pay attention to support mechanisms. The mandates are many, so partnerships must be provided with sufficient resources. Both as a model of process and a symbol of a goal, these conditions can be facilitated through the use of technology.

How Do Technology Tools Help Partnerships?

Throughout partnership building and activity, different technologies can help the process. With different groups of people, with different access to technology, and with different objectives, technology must reflect those realities. Having a clear idea about the ways in which technological tools can be used and developing a repertoire of those tools optimizes their incorporation.

Technology can be divided into resources and production tools. The former include materials such as files, Web sites, CD-ROMs and DVDs, videotapes, audiotapes, and even photos. Production tools include those programs that enable one to manipulate resources and data. Communication tools are a subset of production tools; telecommunications is emphasized in this case. Partners may be considered resources and the partnership as a process. In thinking about technology's role in facilitating partnerships, then, technology as a production tool becomes the focus of attention. Each tool has specific advantages for performing specific tasks.

Desktop Publishing (DTP)

Words still constitute the major means of communication, and the written word remains the mainstay of documenting ideas. With the advent of DTP, the appearance of these publications has been greatly enhanced. When a basic word processing program is opened, it automatically gives the user several format options: memos, letters, brochures, directories, newsletters, even legal pleadings. In addition, the user can save a document as a Web page almost as easily as a text file.

One key to successful written communication is planning. When a document is produced collaboratively, front-end work should be planned. Consider the following when planning a document:

- *Have a clear objective and message in mind.* Are you letting people know what's going on in a program? Trying to recruit people? Showcasing student work? Each objective shapes the content and the tone of the communication.

- *Determine the time frame.* Is the objective short term or long term? A campaign, for example, needs a different approach than an ongoing presence. For the former, a set of flyers and brochures can do the trick; for the latter, a periodical publication makes the most sense. A monthly four-page newsletter can be ambitious for small groups. It is better to produce a two-pager monthly than a quarterly four-pager; it is more timely and gets the message out more often—and there is less to digest.

- *Identify resources.* The type and quality of a publication depend on money, personnel, equipment, distribution needs, and time. If groups have strong editors and designers—or can pay for them—they can probably produce more sophisticated pieces. Access to high-end technology can also result in finer publications—as long as the producer can take advantage of the special features. Large runs can mean lower per-piece costs, but the overall price will still be higher than for a few copies. Of course, fancier does not mean better. Sometimes the bells and whistles can obstruct the message, which should be the driving force.

- *Select the type of publication.* For immediate impact, try flyers and posters. For in-depth analysis, develop detailed reports. Frequently asked questions (FAQs) can be answered in guidesheets and brochures. Produce periodicals for ongoing communication.

- *Determine responsibilities.* Who has the skill and the resources? What has the greatest impact? Who has the most to gain? Collaboration benefits publications: One group may have financial backing and the other personnel with specialized skills or a greater amount of time for labor-intensive work. Each step of the publication should be determined in terms of material resources, personnel, and time—for submission, editing, distribution, and steps in between. A sophisticated document may need a long lead time, whereas a simple notice can be done quickly. The faster the turnaround time, the more timely the information; any bottleneck along the way can spell disaster.

- *Know the reader.* For elementary students, use lots of visual cues and lively writing. For teachers, make the document practical and supportive of their efforts. For the community, include tips for helping their children and improving their own lives. In some cases, a variety of publications might be developed for the same goal, each one targeted to a narrow group.

- *Set the tone visually.* Two columns are usually less formal than three. A "ragged" right edge is less formal than a right-justified margin. A narrow white column gives a contemporary look. Lines between columns look formal; white space between is lighter; dotted lines between columns can be fanciful. Usually, the more formal the message is, the fewer graphic elements should be included. Photos are great, but even clip art can be a welcome change for the eye. In most cases, put captions with the photos, especially to credit that special person and the photographer. However, beware of too many graphics or shadings; they create a "noisy" and confusing look. The look should be cohesive to provide a consistent message. When working together on a newsletter "look," all partners must agree on the visual template or agree to go along with the decision of the layout editor.

- *Note article placement in newsletters.* The upper right-hand corner has the highest visual impact, so place your most important message on the front page in that corner. A good place to put a table of contents is at the bottom of the sidebar column or in the lower right-hand corner if there isn't a sidebar column. The verso (left) page is a good place for editorials or longer, more serious pieces. If more than one group is writing for the newsletter, regular page allocations should be determined from the start. Leave space in the lower third of the fourth page to place an address label.

- *Create a standard look in terms of fonts, headlines, and style for a series or set of documents.* Consider using a consistent logo for all publications.

Databases

By partnering, libraries can subscribe to electronic databases more cost effectively. However, the real strength of joint ventures is in the creation of local databases that would be hard to duplicate elsewhere. Particularly in these days of value-added service, customized databases provide worthwhile, hard-to-find information in an organized, accessible way. When creating a database, consider the following questions:

- What is the objective of the database? To provide teens with community resources? To link people to job opportunities? To offer a speakers' bureau? Usually, groups begin by determining what kind of information is needed that cannot be found easily in one place or by identifying unique resources or services within the community.

- How will the database be used? The answer determines the fields and the index. A database of historical landmarks might be sorted by age, street, or architect. A community needs assessment, or at least a thorough discussion among partners, should occur early to verify the information needed. Creating a pilot database enables partners to test the fields and sorting protocols so that they reflect desired outcomes.

- What database program will be used? All parties should be able to use the information. Check to see if files can be converted into available programs if participating groups use different software. Ideally, databases should be relational so files can be merged and repurposed in conjunction with existing data for other objectives.

- How will data be gathered and input? Standard procedures must be established, and responsibilities should be clearly delineated. If more than one person does this work, unambiguous documentation and training are imperative. In addition, all data must be verified as well as maintained.

- Who will access the data? This is an important question, particularly if the process to create the database is costly; those costs must be recovered somehow. For the school library, such a database might be considered a public service, with the expenses absorbed by the school or the collaborating partner. A custom database might be the benefit of membership to an organization. If the information does not change frequently the database might be copied and distributed as a fund-raiser. The decision depends on the partners' agreement.

Spreadsheets

A spreadsheet is a particularly useful data manipulation tool because it allows the user to structure data in a clear format and to perform different mathematical operations on data to interpret them statistically. The data can be entered and modified, stored, and printed for effective use. Spreadsheets can be used by partners for reports, statistical analyses, budgets, and other management operations. Among the potential applications are the following:

Joint collection development: By testing different cost configurations, library media teachers calculate processing and cataloging costs in the manner of zero-based budgeting to arrive at more representative figures.

Space management: Allocating space is facilitated by using spreadsheets. By estimating the number of items per shelf and determining the section dimensions and aisle space, library media teachers can compare different facilities and their arrangement for shelf arrangement. Parent groups may be thinking of developing a separate resource center for parenting materials; presenting them with a spreadsheet analysis may demonstrate that it would be more cost effective to house such a specialized collection in the school library.

Staffing: Several personnel issues can be examined via spreadsheets. Professional and paraprofessional tasks can be examined by looking at time use and service outcomes. In another vein, by calculating staff cost for services rendered, the library media teacher can determine cost-back fees for partners.

Library standards: The public library output measures and *Information Power* documents offer great opportunities for spreadsheet applications. Most descriptive and inferential statistics lend themselves to spreadsheet format. Patterns of use can be determined by looking at ranges, typical use, grouping, or variance of figures. Do significant differences exist among types of users or services? Inferential questions like this can be answered with appropriate formulas in spreadsheets. Various factors may affect media center and partnership effectiveness: patron age or gender, donations versus purchases, format of information. As long as the measurement is clearly categorized, statistical operations using spreadsheets are feasible.

Graphs: Many spreadsheet programs enable the user to generate impressive graphical representations. These visual representations can be very effective for group presentations.

Presentation Programs

PowerPoint presentations have become de rigueur these days for conferences and other meetings. Presentation tools make it easy for anyone to organize key concepts and illustrate them through graphics, hyperlinks, or other media. When partners develop these presentations, they help convey standard messages to their constituents. Complex products can be produced as each group prepares its own section and melds it with the others. Of course, such cohesiveness demands thorough planning. Some planning tips follow:

- Storyboard the entire project ahead of time and agree on details such as layout, color, and font as well as the shape of the content and tone of delivery.

- Check equipment and software versions to ensure that all files can be easily transferred. Consider corollary products such as Web broadcasts of the presentation, CD-ROM distribution, and poster displays.

- Determine who will provide the content and who will create the product. It is probably a good idea to have one design person to coordinate the effort to ensure a unified look.

Telecommunications

Listservs, newsgroups and e-mail address books all provide a means for groups to share information efficiently in a relatively secure environment. Groups and individuals can use telecommunications as they solve problems, plan, carry out projects, and mentor. Graphic and text files can be shared, so each party can make modifications or comments, marking their contributions. Both synchronous and asynchronous communication facilitate group work, accommodating individual constraints and preferences. Most telecommunications channels also archive the discussion for future documentation as needed. At the upper end, videoconferencing enables participants to see each other and support documents in real time. Although most people are becoming comfortable with telecommunications, keep the following in mind:

- Gear the telecommunications channel to the lowest level of equipment available in the group. Some machines cannot support Java script. Some systems crash when using high-level graphic chat programs. When in doubt, cut-and-paste files rather than use attachments (or use .pdf files) to avoid conversion problems.

- Try to use telecommunications as the main means of communication and file transfer, and help every person get an e-mail account. Snail mail should be available if needed to ensure equitable access to information.

- Encourage users to keep prior messages to form an ersatz threaded discussion. This practice allows participants to understand the trains of thought as projects develop.

- Videoconferencing requires more thorough planning, to set up connections (particularly when several sites go online simultaneously), ensure that equipment is compatible, and obtain possible technical assistance. Videoconference topics should be well structured, with designated moderators and questioners. Use visuals to break up segments and provide relief from constant "talking heads." Careful attention must also be paid to the receiving end so all participants feel like part of the action.

World Wide Web

The Internet provides a rich communications environment. Used as either an intranet to facilitate in-house work or an extranet to extend services to the larger community, documents on the World Wide Web have the added features of graphics, sound, motion, and hyperlinks. In addition, materials can be read by both personal computers and Macintoshes; the limiting factors are modem speed and sophistication of the browser. The Web also serves as an efficient way to manage knowledge: the collective expertise of the partners. When developing a Web site collaboratively, remember the following tips:

- As in other collaborative efforts, identify the objective and audience of the Web site and decide what resources to allocate to the project. These touchstones will help determine the content and appearance of the site. Groups may decide to produce separate Web sites with links to each other or to develop a joint site to highlight collaborative efforts (and include links to their respective sites farther down in the page). Each approach sends a different message.

- Create a template and regular deadlines for submissions to ensure consistency and timeliness. Make sure that all graphic elements can be transmitted and read easily; use .jpg files for photos and .gif files for line drawings.

- Some typical items found on public Web sites are FAQs, staff/personnel, location information, calendar, news, publications, archives, related links, and contact information. Develop the unique features of the collaboration rather than trying to be all-encompassing.

- Consider developing a dynamic site that allows for easy updating of individual portions of the site. Sophisticated scripting facilitates user searching and site archiving.

- Use the Web as a training tool. Online guidesheets work as references for procedures. A page of hot links to other tutorials shortcuts searching for relevant online training. WebQuests provide interactive training through links to good sites and follow-up activities.

Digitized Images

A good collection of pictures and video clips offers attractive additions to public relations publications. Although digital cameras and camcorders speed up importing images, good software can also transform traditional photos (via scanners) and analog videotapes (via iMovie and other editing programs). In addition, film can now be developed digitally and transferred onto disk or e-mailed to the creator. Graphics programs such as PhotoShop enable the user to modify and combine images for effective incorporation into documents. To facilitate sharing, have one person in each group act as the point person to archive and send the images. An interesting option is to create a CD of images and clips that can be edited and used for different purposes.

Caveats about Technology

Technology can be considered as an end as well as a means. However, the choice to incorporate technology must always involve the ultimate goal of the partnership. If technology furthers the plan, and does so cost effectively, then use it. On the other hand, if it creates barriers or sidetracks the partnership, reconsider its use.

Although technology can bring people closer together through speedy sharing, it can also create distance because of its abstractness. Those implicit messages sent through body language are lost when transmitting through bits and bytes. If for no other reason than difficulties in typing, conversation can become more stilted, less spontaneous. Therefore, every effort should be made to form positive relationships face-to-face before going online. Consider meetings as benchmark events and online collaboration as a constant updating process.

The technology is only as good as its weakest link, so when partners use technology, both parties must update software and hardware concurrently—or be prepared to share information at the lower level. In some cases, one partner may provide the needed upgraded technology while the other partner can provide other resources such as personnel or facilities. Not only must the equipment be "in synch," the expertise to handle the newest versions must also be planned accordingly. Training should include the relevant individuals from each group.

Individuals and groups may have different comfort levels with technology. Using Maslow's (1968) hierarchy of needs, one can map technology needs:

Physiological: access to resources, technical support, and training, technology infrastructure, technology play

Safety: confidentiality, policy and administrative support, sense of safety, technical safety need and maintenance

Belonging: partnerships, coaching, interaction

Esteem: competence, recognition, leadership roles, mentoring

Self-actualization: innovation, creative application

Before higher levels of technology are incorporated into partnerships, the lower levels must first be addressed.

Community Management

One of the hottest topics in technology is "community management": maintaining online groups. As with face-to-face operations, good online communication increases group stability and productivity. Online communities refer to interactions between a host group and participants. In a business scenario, participants could be customers or suppliers. Partnerships lend themselves well to this electronic model. Activities involved in online communities include special events, partner-generated content, regular interaction, and outreach. Online community managers should coordinate planning, monitoring, and rewarding contributions—in timely response to community needs and changes.

Alan Warns, COE of Participate.com, a manager of online communities, identifies three core and four supporting elements in community management (Warns, Underberg & Cothrel, 2000). *Program creation* deals with the objectives and processes unique to the community. Software must be identified to support these activities, such as online chat and Web hosting. *Execution* depends on sufficient technology and human expertise. For example, because interactivity is paramount, dynamic updating must be ensured so content can stay fresh. *Iteration* presupposes that, as a community grows and changes, online management can scale up accordingly. When the online infrastructure can handle this growth, the community itself will benefit more. Supporting processes that provide information to optimize these elements include active listening, interpretation, measurement, and reporting.

Within this arena, *knowledge management* plays an important role. When the implicit knowledge that each person has is shared in a systemic, organized fashion, the organization as a whole benefits. With partnerships, the potential results are even greater. Best practices can be tailored for different groups, policies can be used across organizations, and fund-raising ideas can be coordinated in partnerships. Various technology tools provide the means for knowledge management across groups:

Indexing: Contents can be organized for easy retrieval using databases or dedicated products such as MS Office FindFast or Altavista Discovery.

Organizing: Contents can be categorized in hierarchies and networks using VisiMap, MindManager, and PersonalBrain.

Collaborating: Documents can be shared through e-groups or HotOffice.

Web capturing: Web documents can be captured, read, and archived through Webforia's Organizer, Web Whacker, and Web Buddy.

The Web as a whole provides a robust platform on which to mount or link these functions. In community management, one of the key people should be the knowledge manager, a natural fit for the school library media teacher.

One of the newest trends in organizations is leaderless management (Koulopoulos, 2000). According to this approach, no group's "health" depends on one personality. Instead, community identity determines the organization's success. Norms and group rules, along with a strong knowledge base, set the tone for action. In this model, decisions are made based on wide group input. Many professional associations operate in this manner, and partnerships between them also exhibit these characteristics. In online communities, technology helps provide the structure and means to enable such collaborations to succeed.

Close Up

The year-long project described here helped practitioner educators meet the new state technology standard for teachers. The local university college of education partnered with districts it services and with the regional California Technology Assistance Project (CTAP). In this effort, technology served as a means to a technology end.

Developing the Reading Instructional Proficiency of 4th–8th Grade Teachers Through the Use of Technology

The California Technical Assistance Project (CTAP) Region 11, housed within the Los Angeles County Office of Education (LACOE), has been working through teams of content area and technology specialists to develop and implement a new series of resources that will help teachers to increase their students' levels of achievement. This proposal will enhance that work by partnering LACOE with the California State University–Long Beach (CSULB), School of Education. This new partnership will lead a professional development program of 120 hours. The program will develop teachers' instructional technology proficiencies, knowledge of the CA reading standards, and ability to use the new technology resources within a standards-based instructional design, with a focus on 4th–8th grade teachers (including library media teachers and resource specialists) and administrators.

LACOE and CSULB will share project coordination and administration responsibilities. The instruction for all phases of this project will be developed collaboratively by LACOE and CSULB. Reading and technology specialists from local districts will serve as instructors and facilitators where appropriate. The goal of the program will be for all participants to demonstrate mastery of the "Level C" Instructional Technology Proficiencies, within a standards-based curriculum, at the culminating activity for the project. Project evaluation throughout the program will be led by CSULB.

Design Elements of Program

Integration of Technology and Content Standards

This program will further develop the abilities of 100 4th–8th grade teachers (including library media teachers and resource specialists) and administrators, from school districts near CSULB, to utilize new technology and connectivity to deliver standards-based instruction. The goal of the program is to increase teachers' competency with instructional technology, thus enabling them to help students increase their level of achievement of the California Reading Standards. The specific technology skills addressed will include, but are not limited to, the following:

> Analyzing best practices and research findings on the use of technology within instructional design and planning lessons accordingly

> Selecting optimal resources to support, manage, and enhance learning, while considering the specific content to be taught

> Identifying student learning styles and determining appropriate resources for teaching

> Creating and maintaining effective learning environments, using computer-based technology, for a variety of teaching situations

> Applying appropriate measures to ensure security and safety

The content, for all 120 hours of this program, will focus upon, and integrate, two themes. First, instruction will guide teachers in utilizing new electronic resources. These will include presentation, Internet, multimedia, and assessment/diagnostic applications. Second, instruction will allow teachers to utilize their new technology skills within the framework of a standards-based instructional design.

Participants will be given instruction on using online resources (for both PC and Mac platforms) for both instruction and their own ongoing professional development, analyzing and using new digital media, managing classrooms with technology rich environments, tracking and assessing student abilities through diagnostics and data management tools, and implementing new policies and procedures to ensure safety for students. These resources, along with other technology tools, will be integrated into an instructional plan that promotes achievement of the California Content Standards. The overall approach will be collaborative in nature, utilizing a variety of technological tools and other resources. It is anticipated that a broad spectrum of skills will be represented in terms of reading, instructional design, and technology, so peer coaching and support will be emphasized to facilitate the concept of a learning community.

LACOE will guide the integration of technology skills with the content, in conjunction with appropriate K–12 district leadership. Faculty from CSULB will work collaboratively with these K–12 educators to enhance the content of all sessions of this program and to provide guidance in assessment.

Evaluation

The project staff will evaluate the effectiveness of the content at specific stages of the program, based on tools designed and administered by CSULB. Before the intensive initial activity, a series of attitude and behavior measures will be designed for the project. These will be designed for delivery at four key points in the project's activities:

> Pre-assessment during the first day of the intensive initial activity
>
> Post-intensive initial activity
>
> Mid-school year
>
> End of school year and project

The measures designed will need to evaluate the participants' mastery of the key technology skills along with their ability to deliver effective standards-based instruction utilizing technology. Additional evaluation will need to be done utilizing the projects developed by participants. An evaluation rubric will be designed before the beginning of the intensive initial activity and shared with participants during the initial activity.

Delivery System to Be Used

Content During Intensive Initial Activity (45 Hours)

The intensive initial activity will take place over five days during teachers' off-track time. The content during these sessions is designed to evaluate the entering technology abilities of the participants and their knowledge of the content standards. The activities will enable all participants to design a plan for technology integration at their school site and to participate in all follow-up activities. The initial activity sessions will be a mix of didactic technology training, interactive online sessions, and collaborative planning/development time. The goal of the initial activity will be to begin infusing technology into curriculum areas.

Specific lessons and activities for the initial intensive week come from a variety of resources already in use or in development within either CTAP–Region 11 or CSULB. These include:

> Modules from Subject Area Leadership Team training for reading teachers (part of the CTAP–Region 11 RETS plan)
>
> Modules from application-specific training
>
> Assessment and diagnostic tools for reading skills (e.g., Diagnostic Indicators of Basic English Language Skills, self-assessments) and related data management tools
>
> Online collaboration environments (already in use at LACOE and CSULB)

Table: Intensive Initial Activity Schedule

Day 1:	Morning	Technology start-up session with research/reactions on reading and on technology benefits; initial assessment of technology skills and deficiencies.
	Afternoon	Standards overview (California frameworks/standards, CTC technology standards, ISTE student technology standards, AASL information literacy standards); discussion of general and subject-specific reading skills
Day 2:	Morning	Internet start-up session—Locating quality digital media, criteria for evaluating quality (examples: NCITE streams); evaluation of software (CSULB supplied)
	Afternoon	Instructional design: examples will demonstrate ways to use technology in reading development (both globally and in terms of subject-specific reading strategies). Development session—short-term lesson plans with assessments (sources: SCORE, etc.)
Day 3:	Morning	Sharing, refining, and analyzing developed lesson plans (rubric designed under CSULB leadership); use of presentation tools
	Afternoon	Modifying lessons to accommodate diverse needs; utilizing technology solutions for classroom management (DIEBELS, NCITE data tools)
Day 4:	Morning	Course analysis; outlining year-long strategic plan to develop student technology skills within standards-based instruction. Need for ongoing assessment.
	Afternoon	Introduction to online collaboration tool/environment. Necessary skills for professional development collaboration (TappedIn, EPSS, E-Groups)
Day 5:	Morning	Final development of year-long goals/plans for technology integration
	Afternoon	Sharing and evaluating developed lesson plans; practice with online collaboration tool/environment.

At the end of the initial activities it will be necessary to determine which participants are at or near the goal "Level C" technology proficiencies. Observation forms, developed under CSULB leadership, will be used during each of the activities in which participants are using computer technology. Instructors will be able to identify the participants exhibiting the goal behaviors at this early stage. The lesson evaluations from all team members will be collected and used by project staff to further determine which participants have truly achieved the Level C Technology Proficiencies at this point in the program.

Content During Follow-up Activities (75 Hours)

Following the intensive initial activity it will be necessary to provide participants with both face-to-face meetings and online sessions that serve to achieve the established goals of the program and respond to any specific local needs that will have arisen during the initial activity. When participants register, they will be given a copy of the CTAP technology standards rubric for self-assessment. Nevertheless, it will be impossible to truly gauge the incoming instructional technology proficiencies of all participants until they arrive at the initial session. For this reason, the content for the follow-up activities is designed with a needed degree of flexibility. The structure of these activities is further described in the "Delivery System" section of this proposal. The content modules for these activities include

- guidance from and access to specialists and experts in reading and technology integration,

- collaboration with teams at different schools,

- sharing of lesson plans that allow students to build technology skills within content standards-based curriculum,

- implementation feedback,

- identifying and responding to individual learning differences through technology tools,

- assessment and data management with technology,

- security and safety policies,

- evaluation of specific roles of technology within a standards-based curriculum, and

- mentoring and guidance on using technology in a variety of student settings (whole class, small group, and individual instruction).

Other modules will need to be developed based on the feedback during each segment of the project. Activities during the initial week will result in new modules developed for follow-up activities, which will lead to a refined design for the mid-year face-to-face meeting, etc. An advisory council of CSULB/CTAP leadership will convene as needed to ensure the quality of all newly developed modules.

Modes of Delivery

Content will be delivered through a combination of large group face-to-face meetings (maximum of 25 participants in each session), online collaborative sessions, and site visits.

Intensive Initial Activity—Face-to-Face meeting (5 days X 9 hours = 45 hours)

The intensive initial activity will take place at designated training labs established through LACOE and a grant from AT&T. One of these labs is located at LACOE while others are located within local school districts. It will be beneficial to utilize 2 labs to allow training of 2 cohorts at the same time. Use of these labs will be provided for this project by that partnership. Instructors for this initial activity will come from LACOE (which already has a technology and reading specialist working with the districts near CSULB), local districts, and CSULB faculty (who can provide leadership on specialized sessions during the week).

Follow-up Activities—Face-to-Face meetings (TOTAL: 30 hours)

The AT&T training labs will also provide a location for additional monthly face-to-face meetings. These days will allow for project sharing, subject matter group discussions, and lessons on delivery of additional content modules. These modules will cover appropriate safety and security policies, methods for identifying and responding to individual differences, and other modules identified by local needs. The weekend conference will also allow for collaboration with teams from other cohorts. (8 days @ 3 hours = 24 hours)

A final End of Project showcase will also be scheduled, using a new location. Participants will be asked to complete evaluations about their own technology plans along with those of other teams in their cohort. The skills required in this evaluation will be the same evaluative skills outlined in the "Level C" proficiencies. (1 day = 6 hours)

Instructors for these two face-to-face components of the follow-up activities will be the same instructors from the intensive initial activity.

Follow-up Activities—Online Sessions (10 sessions X 1.5 hours = 15 hours)

The online sessions will all consist of facilitated, prescheduled 90-minute online collaborations. They will provide a mixture of interactions with content leaders/technology specialists, new technology showcases, or implementation reports and sharing sessions. Instructors and facilitators for these sessions will be hired by LACOE. In addition, some project participants, who will achieve all the Level C technology proficiency indicators during the initial activity, will be identified to serve as leaders and mentors during the online follow-up activities. A system for asynchronous online communication will also be utilized to provide participants anytime access to targeted professional development.

Follow-up Activities—On-Site Meetings (10 visits X 3 hours = 30 hours)

Visits by project staff to team school sites will take place monthly during the school year, bringing entire cohort groups together once a month, with the location rotating among all participating school sites. The purpose of these visits will be for the project staff (both CSULB faculty and LACOE) to share and evaluate site-specific implementation challenges and provide guidance and feedback to participants. LACOE will ensure that one individual is present at all site meetings to ensure continuity.

Collaborative K–12 and University Partners and Contacts Participants —100 Total Participants

This project will serve approximately 90 teachers and 10 administrators from the districts in southeast Los Angeles County. The participants will apply and be selected in teams from individual school sites. Participation from school site administrators, reading specialists, library media teachers, and resource specialists is encouraged. Preference will be given to teams representing a variety of grade levels and entering technology abilities, which include site administrators.

The South East Educational Technology Consortium (SEETC) is an organization of 16 school districts and 2 private schools located in the southeastern part of Los Angeles County. The leadership of this consortium has been involved in the planning of this project and is supportive of its design and goals. It is reasonable to expect that the majority of this project's participants will come from schools within this consortium.

Role of Partners

This project is being developed and guided through a collaborative partnership of the California State University–Long Beach and CTAP–Region 11. Both parties will share responsibility for project administration and content development during all stages of the project. Project management and responsibility for ensuring resources for all project activities (personnel, software, or materials) will fall primarily to CTAP. Overall evaluation of the project and its effectiveness to reach stated goals will fall primarily to CSULB. Within the specific project activities, the roles of the partners are as follows:

Intensive Initial Activity

CSULB—Faculty members will provide content or technology leadership and expertise where appropriate. Faculty will lead and introduce special resources or sessions during the week-long activity.

LACOE—Will provide a cohort leader for each of the four cohort groups. The cohort leaders, working with a project coordinator at LACOE, will secure content and technology specialists to lead sessions within the week. Where appropriate, these specialists will come from existing LACOE staff or district staff within the SEETC consortium.

Follow-Up Activities

CSULB—Faculty will participate in each of the site visits with cohort teams, mid-year weekend conference, and the final culminating activity. CSULB faculty will lead sessions within these activities as appropriate. CSULB faculty will also take part in the online activities, although on a less regular basis.

LACOE—The project coordinator and cohort leaders will ensure that a facilitator is assigned to each cohort for the online follow-up sessions. Where possible this facilitator will be the cohort leader, but this might not be true for all cohorts. The facilitator will be responsible for setting the online agenda with the project coordinator and cohort leader (if applicable) and participating in all online sessions to ensure that project goals are met. The cohort leaders will be responsible for setting the agenda and leading all site visit meetings. In addition, the project coordinator will ensure that specialists for site visits, instructors for mid-year session are arranged from the same group that led the initial activity if possible.

Table: Timeline for Activities

July–August	Planning for initial activity
August 14–18	Initial activity for Cohorts 1 and 2
August 21–25	Initial activity for Cohorts 3 and 4
September 2000–June 2001:	Bi-weekly online sessions: Content and facilitators to be organized by coordinator
September 2000–June 2001:	Site visits—CSULB faculty and LACOE staff visit each school for 3 hours/month
January 2001	Mid-year conference and evaluation
June 2001	Final activity and evaluation

THE NATURE OF GROUPS

"My sixth period class is *so* lively; why can't my other classes be like that?" "Well, you know how *that* committee operates." "That new set of teachers is totally different from last year's crop." These statements all portray the essence of groups: similar characterizations and norms adopted by a number of people. The easiest description is a "label." Be it library media teachers or a clique of students with a specific nomenclature, the label enables individuals to identify one another as members of a group of people with whom they associate. The particulars and complexities of one person are glossed over in favor of generalizations applied to several people. Such practice is not only normal but a survival technique, because instant judgments, or at least assumptions, must be made daily as people interact constantly. Glancing at a group of individuals and being able to assess the relative safety of that group enables one to advance securely along the street or in a mall.

From the inside view, membership in a group has many advantages. If the group enjoys high status, such as high school seniors or Nobel Prize winners, that reputation can "rub off" on a group member. Stating that one is a member of a group facilitates introductions. Membership in the American Library Association, for example, implies that the person is interested in libraries and is probably intelligent and socially responsible. Numbers make a difference too; large projects require the work of many. A protest march of a million typically has greater impact than a sole sign. Consider the leverage of buying power when entire states adopt a textbook series; national labor strikes can be equally influential. At any level, humans have a psychological need to belong to groups.

In the context of partnerships, groups provide a means to "up the ante" for change and improvement. Individuals can participate in advancing a cause, and the power of the group's name alone can influence decisions. The whole can truly be greater than the sum of its parts. To take advantage of that group power requires understanding how groups work. This chapter explains the properties of groups and how to leverage them.

What Is a Group?

A group is a number of individuals who share some commonality, such as "the class of 2004." That commonality is such that non-members can be identified as lacking that quality: the "insider" versus the "outsider." Examples abound: lemon growers versus non-lemon growers, Democrats versus Republicans, girls versus boys. Obviously, different groups overlap; one may be a female Republican orange-grower, for example. However, the group's cumulative characteristics, or one unique feature, distinguish it from another group. Additionally, each group typically has a common goal, such as graduating in the year 2004. Having a mutual objective might in itself be the critical feature of the group.

Members of groups communicate among themselves as individuals and communicate to "outsiders" as a group (e.g., through newsletters, signs, sponsored events). Group members have roles within that entity, be it as an officer or representing a social perspective (e.g., synthesizer, time keeper, gadfly). Effective groups distribute leadership so all members feel valued. When outside pressures challenge a group, members work together to deal with the issue. When problems arise *within* a group, members resolve the difference successfully—or the group disintegrates.

Group effectiveness may be measured along two dimensions: task and social. If a goal is highly valued and the strategies to achieve that goal are both reasonable and challenging, and if those activities truly depend on the support of a number of people, then the group will likely be strong. Likewise, if group members like each other and socialize among themselves a lot, then they too can be considered strong—along that dimension. Although members of a goal-oriented group do not have to spend their leisure time together, and a social group does not have to accomplish great tasks, certainly in those cases where groups have a strong agenda *and* enjoy each other, the impact will be the greatest.

Groups experience different degrees of cohesiveness and depth and change over time. A group might last just one class period, such as a library media center scavenger hunt team. Some groups last generations, such as religious sects. Typically, the longer a group exists, the more stable and substantial it is. However, even a one-year task force may work so intensively and closely together that they constitute a powerful driving force, even beyond their official lifespan. Factors that influence a group's strength include degree of commitment, significance of group activity, effective communication and shared decision making, and group resilience.

Strong groups aren't necessarily better than weak groups, but any partnership should assess the group's characteristics to determine what kind of partnership will be the most appropriate. For example, public endorsement by a national club, such as Rotary Club, can help a school effort even if the club itself is not very active locally. A short-term task force, say one associated with a year-long grant, could be included to optimize impact quickly and provide matching funds. Of course, a strong academic department can offer a good partnership model for other areas of the school and can be leveraged for long-term strategic planning, such as a reading initiative.

Organizational Behavior

Often the library media teacher interacts with an organization. The major differences between a group and an organization are size and complexity. An organization can be thought of as an open system that deals with its environment, taking in and transforming resources. An organization includes several goals and several groups, each of which may differ and all of which are interdependent to some degree (Schein, 1970). Within an organization, several levels of behaviors exist: individual, group, and organizational. Variances within the smaller systems can be tolerated, and organizational-level changes are hard to perceive. The influence of the organization as a whole is significant because a number of entities together leverage resources.

Group Dynamics

At the macro level, groups seem more or less stable, almost static—rather like a rock. The group identity may remain even if membership changes, as does the American Library Association. However, on the micro level, within the group, interpersonal dynamics are abuzz—like molecules spinning incessantly inside that dull-looking rock.

Most groups include two types of roles: official titles and informal influence. The former constitutes the business side of a group: a chair or president, secretary, treasurer, and so forth. Likewise, groups tend to follow set protocols in conducting their business, such as *Robert's Rules of Order* and organizational by-laws. These formal structures facilitate decision making by providing stability and objective lines of communication. Less time is taken up by procedural matters so more constructive work can go on. In terms of organizational behavior, titles represent legitimate power.

However, one would be naïve to ignore the power of informal positions within any group. Typical roles may address task issues or social issues. Roles related to task issues include the following:

The enthusiast

The seeker, who gathers facts and opinions

The expert

The task-master, who keeps the group on focus

The synthesizer, who examines different points of view and sees group trends

The evaluator

The realist/pragmatist

Each of these individuals affects the process of the task to be done.

Roles related to social issues include the following (Johnson, 1997):

The encourager

The listener

The trust builder

The processor, who makes sure that every step is taken

The harmonizer, who tries to keep peace within the group

The communications facilitator

The norm setter, who determines what is acceptable behavior

The problem solver

The clown, who relieves tension

The scapegoat, who is blamed for group malfunctions

When working with groups, or within them, identifying these different roles can help explain how groups reach decisions. Discussing issues with key people *outside* meeting time can facilitate *in*-meeting agendas. For example, once the norm setter is identified, the library media teacher can find out the best approach for asking for group support. Asking the expert in the group speeds the learning curve about an issue. When sounding out the feasibility of an idea, it might make more sense to ask the pragmatist rather than the enthusiast.

The Impact of Technology

With the advent of technology, the nature of groups and their interaction varies more than ever because partners can be virtual as well as physical. Groups themselves can coalesce strictly online, based on mutual interests and needs. Even though they have fewer physical links, each person in a cybergroup still maintains a human identity and has unique resources. In a way, their points of electronic contact act as the group's "glue." Usually these virtual groups meet face-to-face at some point, to provide a physical context, but with videoconferencing and even digitized images and speech, the need for a real group meeting is less.

The same group dynamics exist in cyberspace. However, individuals might assume different roles when using technology. For example, the listener may become the cyber problem solver; the time keeper may become garrulous online. Comfort with technology brings another dimension to the group at the same time that it levels other aspects such as space and time. Leadership may be a factor of who monitors a listserv rather than who displays good ideas and fosters collaboration. Emerging technogroups would do well to start informally using e-mail and interactive chats, only later formalizing telecommunications protocols and roles. At that point, they can then differentiate between operational expertise and group task leadership.

Dynamics Between Groups

Several elements can influence interaction between groups. Hellriegel (1995, p. 247) identifies six key factors: goals, uncertainty absorption, substitutability, task relations, resource sharing, and attitudinal sets.

Goals: Obviously, when goals are clear and mutually beneficial, it is easier for groups to work together. When building coalitions, groups should find overarching common goals to motivate members to partner. Groups also should determine how to make similar goals result not in competition but rather in mutual support. For example, the English department and the library media center staff both want students to become technologically competent. Each group should identify areas of uniqueness to affirm its niche (e.g., technology for analysis versus technology for circulation; lab use versus library media center hardware) as well as areas of mutual effort (e.g., research strategies; helping students find key ideas).

Uncertainty absorption: When groups work together, they make decisions together and share resources. In the process, they must also share control, which can be threatening to either group. Each group must negotiate the balance of power. Which issues will be determined jointly and which will remain with each individual group? How important will those joint decisions be? What will the impact of the decision be? Typical joint decisions include record-keeping procedures, scheduling, and publicity. In general, the earlier in the process joint activities and decisions are identified and negotiated, the easier it will be for the two groups to work together. In terms of technology, one group might be responsible for hosting or developing a Web site and the other group should have some control of content.

Substitutability: To what extent can a person receive services or resources from either group? The extent to which one can call on either group determines its substitutability. An obvious example is circulation: Students can check out materials from the school media center or the public library using the same library card. In team teaching, a student could ask either the classroom teacher or the library media teacher for project assistance. Obviously, for such substitutability to be effective, both parties must agree on the areas of overlap as well as the details of the joint service or resources. Students might be able to access electronic resources in the classroom, in the library media center, or from home—and the resources themselves might belong to the public library or the school media center.

Task relations: Tasks between groups are independent, dependent, or interdependent. Textbooks are one example. In some cases, departments handle textbooks *independent* of the media center. If the media center checks out the textbooks, the department is *dependent* on that media center. If a department checks out textbooks but those materials must first be catalogued and bar-coded by the library media teacher, the two groups are *interdependent*.

Resource sharing: When materials, facilities, or people are shared between groups, careful negotiations must take place to ensure equity and maximize benefits. One such practice that has been done for years but is now gaining in popularity—and controversy—is joint-use libraries by public and education sectors. Who will hire and evaluate staff? Who will develop and maintain the collection? Who will pay for services? How will space be allocated? What will the procedures for technology maintenance be? Each detail must be hammered out, with policies and procedures delineated to ensure equity and accountability.

Attitudinal sets: In some cases, groups may hold stereotypical attitudes about their counterparts. As they get to know each other, they must recognize and surmount those preconceived attitudes. Attitudinal assumptions may facilitate cooperation if positive attitudes about each other jump-start a trusting relationship. On the other hand, negative stereotypes will necessitate placing greater emphasis on proactive beginning events that enable people to get to know each other on a personal level. If competition or conflict arises during the partnership, then it will be harder to achieve mutual goals. Group leaders must constantly check the "vibes" of group members to optimize openness and resolve any destructive conflict early on.

Dynamics between groups vary significantly depending on the nature of the partnership as well as the nature of each group. When partnerships are in name only, usually just the leaders or key representatives are involved. Groups can be quite different with little impact on the partnership. A technology company might give a school some equipment with no strings attached; courtesy thanks and positive publicity are all that may be required.

Group interaction boils down to normative behaviors, with some individual deviations. That is, people act as representatives of their groups, trading "group-speak" values and goals. The stronger the group identity, the more likely it is that an individual will reflect the "party line." In some cases, a group may publish "consistent messages" about core values to help members know what to say to the public or another group. In some larger groups, one person may act as the spokesperson or community liaison to ensure that the group's philosophy is explained consistently. This approach is used to counteract the situation in which an individual may well state the group's policy, then add, "This is the stand of the group; speaking from my own perspective, however, . . ." Such a statement clues the listener in to the group's influence and possible undercurrents not aligned with the group's stated stance.

If groups need to work closely together, such as local business personnel training staff, greater communication and clearer role definitions and differentiations are needed. When a greater number of individuals is involved, greater personal differences in interactive behaviors will arise. In some cases, subgroups may actually become more closely allied than the group as a whole; job counterparts may enjoy a very fruitful symbiosis. In other cases, antagonistic subgroups can undermine the larger effort if overall group identities are ambiguous or weak. For example, if Mac folks and PC advocates cannot reach agreements about software procurements, training technology may be stymied. If the partnership is complex, portions of the plan may progress more rapidly than others. Depending on the degree of individual activity interdependence, variations in group interaction can be reasonably sustained; for example, different departments may be able to get training using different systems.

Life Cycles

Groups, be they partnerships between two people or large organizations, change over time, even if they do not want to. Long-standing organizations may seem static, but they too experience cycles as they begin and evolve; however, because they are so large, that overall change requires years to see. On the other hand, it's easy to experience changes between two individuals. The difference is between redirecting the *Titanic* or a paper boat. The underlying concepts are the same.

One way to think about group cycles is to imagine a campfire (Baron & Greenberg, 1989, p. 264):

> *Form:* At the beginning, groups are tentative and possibly hopeful; think of building that first fire of the day to heat up breakfast. Both the group and the fire need quick, concentrated fuel and close attention. Therefore, both groups and campfires are more likely to get started well if fuel/support are gathered ahead of time. For groups, a concrete activity with immediate impact provides impetus for continued partnerships. This period is crucial; issues of trust, personality, and responsibility must be confronted and resolved. Consider how often beginning fires die out after a few minutes. Identifying key areas for support (fuel) and using a variety of approaches in a timely manner (lighting alternative spots, using different fire starters) are crucial in starting partnerships. People tend to be cautious and polite as they reserve judgment about the group.

> *Storm:* Once the fire or group "takes," more substantial support/fuel is needed. The fire takes form. Groups form norms for behaviors and roles. Conflict is inevitable and must be addressed or it will rankle underground and ultimately destroy group effectiveness. Groups must readjust in light of pressures, be they internal or external. In less successful situations, group norms can be ruptured. Group members may have to do damage control, becoming more sensitive to individual agendas. Otherwise, the group itself may be in jeopardy. In the best of cases, a group becomes more resilient as a result of solving disconnections within itself.

> *Norm:* For the group to make significant progress, it needs a good supply of solid resources with an eye toward sustainability. A mature fire—or group—enjoys the status quo. The emphasis is on maintenance, and group identity is well-established. Although this looks like a strong situation, it can fall into a self-serving malaise.

> *Perform:* Like a strong roaring campfire, groups at this stage are very productive. They have clarified their roles and can tolerate deviations while sustaining their overall image and goals. As long as substantial resources are available, and a group is monitored for broad-brush effectiveness, work can proceed without much tinkering.

> *Re-form:* As the embers die and the goal nears achievement, or membership dies off, the group decides whether to rekindle the flame of its commitment with renewed goals or thoughtfully adjourn—breaking up camp, so to speak.

Technology, particularly as it relates to communication, also changes in accordance with group life cycles. For example, beginning groups need quick response, such as phone and e-mail communication. As the group becomes more established, listservs provide an expedient way to communicate with a variety of individuals. As the group communicates with the outside world with one voice, Web pages are typically developed. For major campaigns, videos may be produced. Mature groups tend to maintain and polish their communications vehicles to sustain currency; they may obtain a domain name or acquire a Web server. Of course, the "earlier" forms of technology still operate, particularly as new members or new goals are incorporated into the group structure.

Power

Within each group power is distributed, sometimes broadly and sometimes narrowly. Although most groups have a leader per se, others provide leadership roles through planning, team building, and follow-through. Most effective groups enable each person to contribute and experience some power. Between groups, power must also be acknowledged and negotiated to sustain a sense of equity.

Power arises from several sources. In a traditional organization, power is bestowed to title holders; this is called *legitimate power*. The idea is that the function reflects the title and reveals the influence of the person with responsibility. Close to this kind of power, *reward power* arises from one's ability to control rewards (e.g., salary increases, promotion); this is usually tied to organizational structures. Likewise, *coercive power* arises from being able to punish (e.g., demote or fire employees). Another source of power is knowledge; this is *expertise power*. This is an effective foundation for school library media teachers. Another set of power bases is founded on personality: *charismatic* and *referent* (e.g., connection to a person in power). This latter category depends on the motivation of the followers as well as on the strength of the individual.

In most organizations, as well as in some larger groups, there is an organizational chart and a power chart. The former displays power in terms of legitimate positions. The latter reflects the realities of how things happen. A group may act much more on the basis of personalities than functions, particularly at the emergent stage. Library media teachers can chart the flow of power by creating a sociogram, similar to the concept of "six degrees of separation." Each circle represents a person or entity; the closer the circles, the closer the association. The main source of power may be drawn at the top or in the middle depending on the organizational culture. Lines also connect people, with the thickness of the line correlating to the strength of the relationship. In either case, the closer one is to the source of power, the more influence one has by association. Thus, by following the lines of power, library media teachers can determine the route by which to gain partners (see Figure 5.1).

The school's culture also reveals how power is shared. This climate indicates what kinds of partnerships, both within and outside the organization, can be established, and what approach to use. Cultures/climates include the following:

> *Exclusion:* This atmosphere harks back to "the good ol' boys" network; definite "ins" and "outs" exist, and transition between the two groups is nigh impossible. In this climate, power is considered as a finite resource; only so much exists, and if one person has more power, then another person has to have less. Basically, partnerships would have to take advantage of whatever social connections exist between leaders in the two groups. Hopefully, one of the two groups will have a more enlightened approach that the library media teacher can work with.

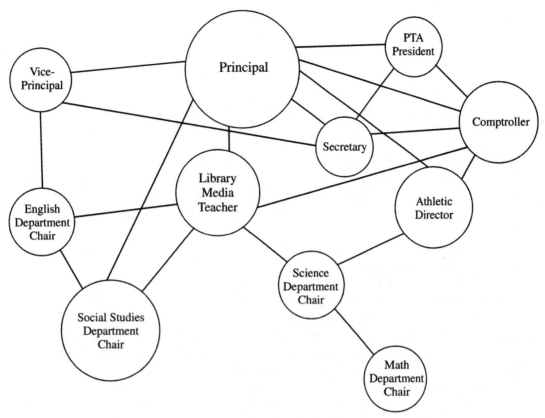

Figure 5.1. Sociogram.

Club mentality: Although cliquish, this atmosphere does not necessarily push down non-members; it just advocates its own way. Any partnership must go along with the "club's" agenda. Fortunately, partnerships do not require total agreement on every point, just one important joint goal.

Compliance: This climate fosters the team approach but may be competitive as well. Outreach to other partners may be supported if it helps the "home team win." As long as partners agree on the rules, they can work together successfully. In this situation, clear expectations up front and consistent communication are musts.

Affirmative action: A conscious attempt to achieve equity exists in this atmosphere; fairness is the touchstone. Although the surface looks good and partnerships can work well on a formal basis, sometimes underlying conflict might be suppressed in an effort to keep everyone calm.

Restructured: Groups reflect on their values and practice as a whole and develop initiatives to address problem areas. As long as partnership action is based on sound data and thought, innovative practice can succeed.

Diversified: Groups with this mentality are the most open and receptive to change and partnerships. They welcome and support innovation and appreciate different perspectives. Partnerships thrive in this atmosphere, particularly because power is seen as limitless. The more that power is shared, the more power is generated.

Large organizations may possess a number of powerful subgroups, so library media teachers should analyze each one and see how they interact.

Groups as Partners

By now it should be well established that teaming with others, particularly groups, enables library media teachers to improve the library media program as well as advance the learning community as a whole. Partners bring resources and expertise as well as new perspectives that can facilitate effective change. They also help evaluate progress as their input triangulates data. Because learning is usually a social activity, partners provide support and encouragement for new ideas. Effective collaborations blend social reinforcement and educational outcomes.

So if partnerships are such a boon, why don't they exist more often—and why do they sometimes fail? First of all, partners must each divest themselves of some control. The traditional "sage on the stage" must share the platform, and both parties probably should "guide on the side." If the partner is an unknown quantity, giving up control constitutes a leap of faith. Partnerships also require time and effort, neither of which exists in abundance. Yet no one person can handle all the jobs required of today's schools; interdependence is the only key to survival, let alone success. As mentioned before, groups should get to know each other in a variety of contexts to build the trust necessary for effective collaboration. Even if collaborations do not exist, school constituents should know each other's business so all activity can be aligned to help implement the school's mission. As for planning, the school culture is a significant defining factor: Is time built in for teamwork, do facilities foster collaboration, is technology in place to facilitate 24/7 communication?

In the final analysis, the library media teacher's own behavior will determine how well he or she interacts with groups and contributes within a group. Each group is composed of individuals, and that personal aspect should never be lost in the transactions. By looking within and aligning efforts with others, library media teachers can reach out and engage with others to improve the school community as a whole.

Close Up

This workshop presentation showed how community-based education can incorporate technology to improve students' lives and the lives of those in the surrounding area. It points out how technology, rather than dividing people, can actually link them as partners and foster equity.

Information Technology for ALL Students: A Presentation on Technology-Based Services to Address Diversity

How Do We Meet Needs of Diverse Students?

Intellectual access to resources

Physical access to resources

Creative, collaborative programs

High-quality library services

Issues of Access:

Race and ethnicity

Limited English proficiency

Poverty

Geographic isolation

How Do ALL California Children Get Equitable Access to Needed Information?

Western states and the Pacific Islands: issues of diversity that must be addressed:

- Less than half of this population is white.

- A quarter of California students is LEP.

- A quarter of this population lives in poverty.

- These same students are likely to be more transient and have less access to vital resources.

Technological Resources

Productivity software

Manipulatives

Internet

Multimedia

Videotape

Productivity Tools

Content-neutral to use across disciplines

Different formats address different learning styles

Open-ended to facilitate creativity

Facilitate student organization and analysis

Help presentation of information

Measure objects

Help analyze surroundings

Help students learn kinesthetically

Internet

Provides worldwide access

Accesses sources in students' primary languages

Combines text, visuals, sounds, movement to address different conceptual "clues"

Connects students of same culture in different lands

Multimedia

Multiple access points to information using different learning modes

Cues to link visual and textual information

Different ways to organize findings

Delivery Systems

Web-based instruction

Video processes

Virtual libraries

Web-Based Instruction

Interactive

Worldwide access (limited by equipment and telephone lines)

Provides learning environment controlled by student

Combines text, sound, graphics, video

Easily updated and improved

Videotape

Instant documentation

Interactive opportunities

Uses skills of oral learners

Promotes collaboration

Can be broadcast worldwide

Virtual Libraries

Intellectual and physical connection to information literacy experts

Access to information

24/7 service through Web interface

Pacific SW Regional Technology in Education Consortium

Deal with these issues through:

    Professional development

    Technical assistance

    Student instructional services

    Collaboration and dissemination

PSR*TEC Programs

Deal with these issues through:

    International student exchanges of projects

    Community-based research

    Distance learning

    Global teaching networks

Global Teacher Network

    "Power of Math"

    "Water, Water Everywhere"

    "Beyond Heroes and Holidays"

Samoan Teen Project

Carson (California), Honolulu, and Samoa:

    Autobiographies

    Videotapes

    Folklore collecting

School-Home-Community

    "Family Connections for School Climate"

    Project Fresca: researching the impact of the strawberry industry on the community

    "Home Talk"

    Cultural packages

Services to Immigrant Youth

    Laptops

    Packaged information

    Mentor teachers

    Cybrarian

Factors for Successful Equity

Effective collaboration among educators

Knowledge about available resources

Technological facilitation

6

BUILDING GROUP PARTNERSHIPS

Although one-to-one partnerships may be the most intense and profound, group partnerships are the norm for in-school library media center cooperation. The library media teacher meets with a department, an age level group of teachers, an administrative council, or another governing body of representatives.

In most cases, the library media teacher acts as the "outside" person, sharing a unique perspective. This person may feel isolated or at least a need to bridge the gap of understanding. As if coming in in the middle of a conversation, the library media teacher may need to be brought up to speed. Here is where advance work in building individual partnerships pays off; the library media teacher can get the inside picture ahead of time from one of the group's members.

In the case of a group of representatives, such as a department chair committee, each person theoretically has an equal say. Because the library media teacher interacts closely with the entire school community daily, he or she actually has a better overall picture than most other staff. On the other hand, because the library media center staff is usually limited in size, the other representatives may underestimate the media center's impact. On that basis, they may question the center's budget, which is usually larger than other constituents' if considered solely in terms of the number of professionals involved in its distribution.

Furthermore, staff may wonder about the library media teacher's ubiquitous presence on various committees that demand representation from each constituency. Again, because the library media center should be the hub of the school, participation in the different meetings is necessary to maintain currency and credibility. Typically, however, the school media center staff consists of one professional and a small support paraprofessional staff, perhaps a part-time clerk or a handful of volunteers. The library media teacher may appear to operate in isolation, having to represent the entire library media center operation as opposed to having a department- or grade-level chair speaking for a block of like-minded educators. When the library media teacher meets with a group, he or she usually goes alone to discuss issues.

However, in a larger sense, the entire media center staff, paid and unpaid, speaks for the library media center. For a significant portion of the school community, whoever works behind the media center desk is considered to be a "librarian." That perception can actually work to the library media teacher's advantage because it helps broaden the base of support. The library media teacher does not have to feel that he or she carries the entire burden of responsibility. Each staff member brings a unique perspective and listens with a unique ear. When media center users have a choice of individuals with whom to interact, they can identify with different types. Additionally, having paraprofessionals represent media center concerns to a governing body can strengthen the media center's sphere of influence. Having student aides on student body councils likewise gives the library media center greater voice in co-curricular affairs. Moreover, volunteers may play an active role in the community and may share their media center experiences broadly, either formally or casually. Of course the key to optimal representation is ongoing communication and an atmosphere of meaningful teamwork.

This spirit of collaboration is valuable throughout the process of establishing and maintaining group partnerships. All library media center staff should be trained in group coalition building. First, the media center staff must be a unified, but diverse, group with agreed goals and aligned strategies. Clear expectations and trusting relationships pave the way to honest, regular communication. Each person should feel responsible for the success of the library media center program and should contribute to its vision and implementation. Because each person brings a unique background and set of skills, couched within a complex personality, the group must develop norms of acceptance and constructive criticism. What habits can be tolerated? What actions undermine the library media center's program? The library media center message must be consistent, but the ways in which that message is addressed can differ. For the group to be functional, the ends must meet, but the means can differ as long as they are aligned. Just as a media center collection represents a variety of ideas but all items are thoughtfully selected to carry out its mission, so must the media center staff model diversity of opinion with unity of mission.

Library media center staff team building provides a model for coalition building that connects with the media center program while sustaining a separate identity. In the ideal situation, the media center staff can be built from "scratch" to optimize a cohesive team. However, in most cases, at least to begin with, media center staffing is done piecemeal, with some individuals well established in the school fabric. In other cases, only one person makes up the media center staff, so such teamwork exists solely in collaboration with volunteers and other supporters. Either way, the nature of the potential team or group depends on identifying existing group dynamics and group goals, meeting with individuals, and then identifying roles within those realities.

Scoping Out the Scene: The Environmental Scan

Whenever strategic planning is done, and particularly when coalition building is part of this planning, the library media center staff should conduct an environmental scan of what is happening around the media center and how it affects the center's program. Table 6.1 contains some examples of information obtained through an environmental scan.

Table 6.1. Environmental Scan

	External Factors	**Internal Factors**
Enhancing	Information society	Strong library media center collection
Neutral	Standards	Student aides
Obstructing	Competing fund requests	Lack of space

External factors are those items outside the media center. *Internal factors* refers to media center matters. Enhancing factors help the media center carry out its program, and obstructing factors take away from the program. Neutral factors may imply no influence or a net zero influence (partly positive and partly negative, but potentially significant). Each item also should be identified as being controllable or not controllable by the library media center staff.

The most important part of this exercise is to take advantage of the environment's positive aspects, aligning efforts to this end. In those happy situations where the library media center can join—or lead—the bandwagon of the Information Age and other affirmative societal trends, the power of those larger issues creates a halo effect that facilitates media center action. Conflicting trends beyond the media center's control, such as an economic recession, should be recognized rather than ignored, especially if they can affect the media center program. In the example shown in Table 6.1, the media center might find its budget or staffing in risk of being reduced, so the library media teacher should build a stronger case for sustaining present levels of support or may need to seek alternative sources of help. In the worst-case scenario, the library media teacher may need to prioritize and reallocate program needs to minimize negative impact.

Environmental aspects that the library media center can control or influence become the focus of attention because there effort can be rewarded. Those positive aspects, such as a strong reference collection, require attention to maintain their healthy level. Other school community members look at the media center's efforts in these areas to see if it is doing its core work and making effective use of its resources and favorable status. The underlying message is to make good use of what you have or you won't have anything to make use of.

Getting Group Support

Regardless of the type of partner or its relative power, certain steps facilitate the establishment and support of partnerships. When library media teachers have to work from a relatively small power base, they should work thoughtfully to garner support.

- *Build from strength.* Library media centers must have strong programs, and library media teachers should be responsible, credible, and professional. They should build up resources and competencies so they will attract partners and have something to contribute to others.

- *Learn about the potential partner.* Make personal contact. Learn the partner's jargon and understand the partner's agendas and values. Get involved. Attend meetings. Ask questions.

- *Share resources and expertise.* Educate each other. Find out the partner's needs and help satisfy them. In turn, ask for help based on analysis of what the partner can offer easily.

- *Take risks.* Go the extra mile. Get out of the library media center's comfort zone. A bit of a challenge offers the greatest chance for learning and partnering. This attitude also models the kind of action desired on the part of the other party.

- *Form a partnership or coalition.* Find a common goal or overarching issue that both parties can address together and leverage to a greater extent through joint effort. From this point, in-depth planning and implementation can occur.

When choosing potential partners, library media teachers should consider several factors:

Goals and values: What is the group's agenda? How closely does it align with the library media center's?

Reputation: How is the group viewed by the rest of the community? What is its track record as a separate entity and also as a partner?

Resources and competencies: What does the group offer? Does it complement or support media center resources and library media teacher skills?

Power: How important is the group's participation? To what extent is the library media teacher's power useful to the group?

Climate: How easy is it to partner with the group? Has a partnership already been established with the group?

Uniqueness: How crucial is this group; can another group be chosen just as well?

Library media teachers should not leap into partnerships just for the sake of joining a group. The fit must be good, and the collaboration should advance the media center program as well as the school community. Of course, the library media teacher might be asked to serve on a committee that seemingly has little to do with media center matters, such as a union negotiating team, but in most cases such teamwork helps build library media teacher credibility and paves the way for other partnerships with more obvious connections to the media center. (By the way, union representation is a powerful way to understand school dynamics, and it can affect library media center staffing.)

Planning

Once library media teachers connect with others, they can start thinking about actually collaborating with them. Within the scope of the learning community, the library media center itself might not be considered the center of the universe, so the library media teacher must abandon a possibly myopic point of view to embrace the goals of the larger community. When those overarching goals align with the media center's, then all partners benefit.

The California State Department of Education offers a fine planning model (http://www.cde.ca.gov/ctl/edtechplan.pdf) that can be adapted to establish and optimize partnerships to improve the school community, particularly in light of technology. It emphasizes the need to identify key constituents, access needs, and "plan the plan."

Get Started

Initial steps lay the foundation for the rest of the process. Just as a child's first experiences are the most important because they cannot be judged in light of other experiences, so do first efforts in establishing partnerships set the tone for future work. Thus, extensive preparation and support are vital. Grassroots and individual initiatives can foster growth, but an effective leader with a clear vision really must set an example and provide the means to garner initial support. Often, a strong school has strong leadership, and that combination attracts key stakeholders.

Of course, the challenge is to identify appropriate partners. Attraction is not enough; rather, the goal is a good match between partners based on mutual goals and supportive resources. As a community entity, the school leadership should be able to identify good prospects. The school library media teacher should also maintain strong links with the community. That mindset, along with the ability to conduct research effectively, positions library media teachers as key people in determining likely partners. Those partners can then be recruited, presumably by school leadership.

If technology constitutes an integral part of the partnership, either as a means or as an end, partners must be able to support technology accordingly. In partnerships, all parties must identify how infusing technology benefits the plan. A base of technological resources and expertise must be available, but partners need not limit themselves to the technology status quo; improving technological aspects of each party can become part of the plan—and the benefit.

The core planning team should decide what procedures to use in planning. Who will lead? What role will each partner play? What task groups need to be established? What will be the lines of communication? When conflict arises, how will it be resolved? Clarifying these expectations and norms for partnerships facilitates future activities.

Once the essential partners and procedures are in place, the overarching vision and supporting mission statement can be developed. The role of technology should also be articulated.

Start Planning Activities

The next step is to bring other members of the partnership on board and to identify other relevant groups. The mission can be shared with this larger constituency, laying the groundwork for broad-based support. If technology plays a key role, then its present status and potential should also be shared with the community.

The group as a whole can develop the game plan: tasks, strategies, timelines, benchmarks, and responsibilities. As part of the planning process, the group should determine how to document and communicate its steps. Project management software programs facilitate this stage. In fact, it makes sense to incorporate and systemize GroupWare or telecommunications-based collaboration tools at this point. A good way to start using these technology tools is to brainstorm potential community partnership resources and funding. Technology facilitates cyberspace communication and electronic recording.

Assess the Current Status

Although partners may know where they want to go, they must first determine where they are. This information becomes baseline data from which to measure progress. To accomplish this task, the planning team has to identify the appropriate assessment tools:

- What will be assessed: student achievement, school resources, faculty expertise, community needs, constituent attitudes?

- Who will do the assessing: students, staff, parents, the community? Ideally, at least two constituents should assess to determine to what extent point of view influences perception.

- What assessment tools will be used: surveys, focus groups, observations, standardized tests, content analysis, user patterns? The tool should align with the objective and take into consideration available resources. For example, parent focus groups might be hard to arrange on short notice; however, if a school extranet is actively used, then getting parent input might be easy.

- When will the assessment be conducted: once or several times; at the beginning, middle, or end; at benchmarks?

- How will the assessment be used: to identify needs, to determine and allocate resources, to measure progress, to modify the plan?

Technology should be assessed in terms of skills and attitudes, current software and hardware, networking capabilities, facilities, curriculum alignment, training, support, and funding levels and sources.

Identify School Improvement Efforts

Any plan, but especially one that involves community partners, must align with other school initiatives. If is works in isolation, its impact on student learning will be minimal. Schools routinely juggle a number of priorities, so the planning team must see how their plan ranks in comparison with other projects, as well as how it supports other endeavors. A basic rule of thumb is: "Use existing structures; make them work for you."

First, the team should identify site and district administration priorities. If the partnership's plan aims to incorporate technology into the school culture, how might technology help further those administrative issues—or possibly conflict with them? Obstacles and opportunities should be uncovered and resolved. What parts of the plan can be done first to lay the groundwork for the rest of it?

Next, the team should look at school curriculum initiatives in terms of their relationship to the plan. Again, where do natural alignments occur? What areas lend themselves to immediate action? Either a key issue or an easy issue should be tackled first to demonstrate a concrete difference quickly to the school as a whole.

Because school staff constitute the main force for school improvement, the planning team should work with staff to determine their needs. Otherwise, the project will be undermined and staff morale will take a dive. Already, schools have to deal with increasingly high-stakes standards, sometimes with no additional resources or training or time to "ramp up" instruction and achievement. If, for example, students must meet technology standards, it makes sense for each classroom to have student-accessible computers with Internet access; if that resource is not available, that could well be the project's first priority. If Internet access is the bottleneck because the school is not networked, then *that* action should be prioritized. On the other hand, teachers might not have been trained in ways to examine course work in light of technology enhancements; in this case, staff development time should be carved out to facilitate that critical review.

Of course, one key to successful action is effective communication. Again, existing means of communication should be identified and used for the project. How is information about other initiatives being shared? Can the partnership project be incorporated into those missals? Perhaps communication lines are not optimal; the project can be leveraged to address that problem and thus gain credibility. By looking at the flow of information—and the bottlenecks—the team can maximize relationships with other successful initiatives and clear the way for trouble-free communication. In effect, this procedure is part of knowledge management. After investigating these school infrastructure matters, the planning team can couch its project in terms of schoolwide improvement when it reports to the community at large about the proposed plan.

Systemize Technology Support

Analyzing the needs of school constituents leads to developing appropriate and effective supportive technology systems. Some improvements address schoolwide issues; others deal with specific gaps. For instance, networking a school site affects administrative as well as instructional coordination and communication. Likewise, agreeing on one suite of productivity software and developing standards for equipment donations facilitates cross-group efforts. A regular schedule of maintenance and upgrading also should be put in place.

On the other hand, each constituency probably has specialized technology needs. Administrators need student-tracking software. Teachers need grading programs. Library media teachers need cataloging/circulation programs. Special education requires assistive technology. Specific curricula require graphing calculators, science probes, multimedia production software, and so forth. If school initiatives include outcomes-based learning and authentic assessment, they will probably require exploring the use of electronic portfolios. In that case, instructional servers should include space for students to store their work, and student-accessible systems will require high-capacity storage devices such as Zip drives or CD-R/W drives so students can collect and index their sample work throughout their educational lives.

But technology resources do not affect student performance; effective instruction does. Therefore, staff members need adequate training and technical assistance for whatever systems and software are introduced into the school. Before any plan can be implemented, staff members must be assessed to see what training they need and determine the preferred way to get that training. Some people like manuals and guidesheets; others prefer videotapes. Some like learning at home; others enjoy working in groups at school. Because of prior experience and learning differences, individual needs must be considered. School staff typically reflect a wide range of abilities and interests. The more that affinity groups can form with staff choice, the more likely it is that mutual support will speed up learning. Because initiatives go beyond the status quo, every effort must be made to facilitate that transition.

The organization of human interaction also should be analyzed in terms of technological facilitation. For example, teachers may ignore mailroom flyers or may not have joint planning time. If every teacher is supplied with a free e-mail account and accessible networked computer, announcements can be broadcast in a timely manner and teachers can e-mail each other about lessons. If Group-Ware is installed on the school server, accessible to all staff, documents and projects in general can be reviewed in common more easily.

Based on the analysis of technological needs, the planning team can then determine associated costs, not only of materials but also of personnel. They can prioritize expenses and develop a reasonable timeline for addressing these different issues. This step becomes part of the overall planning matrix.

Develop the Implementation Plan

Finally! How do all these great ideas become reality? Sometimes it seems that planning is a self-recursive process. Yet how the project rolls out greatly affects its impact. In general, a short-term, concrete project provides the foundation for longer-term, more substantive work. Once partners feel successful on a small scale, they are more willing to build on that strength and reach out and upward.

Whatever the plan's scale, however, the community should have the capacity to support the project. The following procedures should be detailed in terms of costs to be incurred, staffing, and training:

> Software acquisition, installation, and use
>
> Hardware and networking acquisition, installation, and facilities management
>
> Technology standards, policies, and procedures development and scheduling
>
> Staff development and support coordination
>
> Knowledge management to facilitate communication and improvement cycles
>
> Fund-raising coordination

For example, personnel training requires not only personnel but also time and coordination. As with any other type of instruction, staff development must consider the objectives, trainers, resources, delivery system, assessment, and followup.

Assess and Revise the Plan

How well does the plan work? Have the goals been met? Do students succeed? Too often more emphasis is placed on input and interventions than on output or impact. Particularly with a partnership-based plan, each portion affects the other; it can be hard to deconstruct a complex system to identify specific areas of strength or need. Yet if the assessment tools and processes are identified ahead of time, analysis can be done systemically.

A key to success is ongoing partnership communication and review—and redirection or modification of the plan. The team members also must share their findings, recognize achievement, and celebrate progress with all participants and supporting stakeholders.

When a plan incorporates technology, such tools should be used in the assessment and communication. Online tests and surveys help gather data. Spreadsheets and databases help organize and synthesize data. Statistical tools such as SPSS help disaggregate data to find meaningful patterns. Collaborative tools facilitate feedback. Telecommunications and video help spread the word. Technology use by the planners is a model for technology use by those affected by the plan.

TEAMING WITH SCHOOL MEMBERS

The school community itself reflects a complex set of partnerships engaged in helping young people learn and achieve. Individuals and groups within the school represent a wide variety of attitudes and competencies, hopefully all aligned with the school's mission. Within this community, the school library media teacher can serve as a catalyst to bridge different perspectives and help coalesce efforts.

The Varieties of Power

Because the school is involved in so many activities, a monolithic approach to power is unrealistic. It is true that, in terms of organizational structure, function-based power, or authority, is relevant. Usually the principal is the Chief Executive Officer (CEO) of the institution and is backed by other administrators. Department- or grade-level chairs supervise their colleagues. However, power can arise from other factors such as seniority, association with legitimate power figures (e.g., the principal's golfing partner), popularity, or control (e.g., the business manager).

Moreover, for any specific project or school agenda, power and leadership may change. Each committee may have a different chair. Over the course of implementing a school initiative, staff may change—and so might the dynamics of power. Even personal changes, such as marriage or family status, can affect the amount of time that can be dedicated to school issues and change the balance of power within a group.

Typically, potential partners are identified in terms of their "normal" function or title. The list usually includes teachers, support staff, administrators, and students. Teachers may be subdivided by subject matter, grade level, or administrative function (e.g., department chairs). However, potential partners may also be identified according to activity or committee, such as Site Council, student activities, staff development, or reading initiative.

Library media teachers should discern how they are viewed by the rest of the school community. In this author's survey of southern California schools (Farmer, 2000a), the school community asserted that the core function of the library media teacher is to be an information specialist: acquiring, organizing, and making resources available in support of the curriculum. So the library media teacher who charges out ahead waving information literacy standards in front of teachers' noses may not get a welcome response; more likely, that library media teacher—and the message—will be ignored. The library media teacher should use that core value to open the door to collaboration. The image and influence of the library media teacher too may change, so partnerships can act as a way to facilitate empowerment.

When establishing partnerships within the school, the library media teacher must be aware of changing spheres of influence. This approach can be liberating because it recognizes that a variety of people can contribute significantly to the well-being of the school, and that the act of partnering itself can help individuals or groups gain power in the school community. Library media teachers should take a deeper look at how different constituents work and match the project at hand with the most effective resources available.

Teachers

Beyond the library media center staff itself, classroom teachers are the logical first partners for the school library media teacher. Too often, teachers and library media teachers do not work together—or even in tandem. Typically, teachers see themselves as the instructional leaders, even in terms of information literacy, and see the library media teacher as their support. Library media teachers cannot serve the school community well, and students in particular, without collaborating closely with teachers. Because today's classroom teacher remains the key formal educator for children, the library media teacher must go the extra mile to assess the teacher's needs and support classroom efforts. To that end, library media teachers should speak each teacher's lingo and understand each teacher's environment.

The following strategies can help the library media teacher become involved in daily education and smooth the way for effective collaboration:

- Examine relevant standards and frameworks, curricula, assignments, textbooks, and student work.

- Visit classes. Talk with students and parents.

- Volunteer to help grade student work, even if just to check bibliographies.

- Display student work in the library media center and lend posters and artifacts for class displays.

- Share good resources, both print and nonprint, with teachers—tying them to their curriculum.

- Maintain a professional collection, including Web sites.

- Read professional journals in the teachers' areas of expertise.

- Develop an e-mail address book "grid" by grade level and subject matter, and flag new resources (both in the library media center and on the Internet) for teachers.

- Coach teachers on Internet use: locating, evaluating, and using electronic sources.

- Share information about copyright and plagiarism; create WebQuests on these topics.

By building on their core areas of expertise, library media teachers can gain credibility in the teaching arena. They can then form partnerships that expand on those roles and enrich student learning through enriching teachers' repertoire of tools and approaches. Following are some beginning collaborative projects that incorporate technology:

- Design a school Web page of student, teacher, and parent resources.

- Develop a schoolwide database of favorite student reading.

- Develop a database of community speakers.

- Develop a database of technology-enhanced products, with fields sorted by software program, subject, grade, and so forth.

- Design a scope-and-sequence for information literacy (incorporating technology standards).

- Develop a collection of student exemplars to ensure consistent grading of portfolios.

- Videotape and archive best practices.

- Develop a knowledge management database to share best practices.

In the lower grades, the teacher has the same set of students most of the day and must design and carry out meaningful learning activities every day. Those teachers get to know their students very well, continuously assessing them and individualizing instruction almost unconsciously. Primary teachers, especially, need to know all subject matter and have a strong sense of child development to develop appropriate lessons; most try to create thematic experiences to help children contextualize their learning. At this level, classrooms tend to be smaller, and teachers may well have instructional aides or parent volunteers to provide individual attention. Although such help is welcome, it imposes another burden on the teacher because he or she must train and supervise these extra hands. In terms of administration, grade-level teacher groups tend to be the governing structure. Articulation between grades is important, but consistency within the same grade is more pressing.

Knowing these specific factors about elementary schools, library media teachers can maximize their impact by applying some of the following techniques:

- Approach the grade-level coordinator and ask to attend his or her meetings.

- Develop model collaborations with classroom "teams": teacher, aides, parent volunteers, technology specialist, and special education teacher.

- Train parents in information literacy skills and have them work with individual teachers.

- Show how technology can help teachers' productivity, for example, the use of personal device accessories (PDAs) to assess student learning just-in-time.

- Approach information literacy on a grade-by-grade basis.

- Develop information literacy articulation by identifying existing cross-grade groups such as Site Council and using grade-level work as a starting point for seamless student developmental learning.

As the grades advance, teachers increase their depth of subject understanding and narrow their subject range. Middle school teachers are likely to teach students in "blocks" of time, linking language arts and social science or mathematics and science. Even subject-specific teachers tend to collaborate with their academic "siblings" so student assignments can leverage each other's skill domain. Thus, students may learn genetics at the same time that they learn mathematical probability. In middle school, project-based learning is a popular way for students to learn because it involves a variety of learning styles and concretizes concepts. At this point, students start to take ownership of developing and assessing personal portfolios of learning evidence to show progress. These approaches to education require that middle school teachers develop ways to keep track of student competencies linked to content standards across disciplines and classes. They also have to teach students how to assess their own work and each other's.

At this level, the library media teacher might do well to use the following strategies:

- Work with teacher teams within each grade.

- In those cases where middle schools adopt a schoolwide theme, such as "earth stewardship," participate actively in those curricular coordination efforts.

- Archive projects for future reference.

- Research information literacy-related rubrics and help teachers and students use them.

- Develop a schoolwide database of information literacy skills linked to each student.

By high school, schools tend to be run along department lines. Students take one to four years of different subjects, keeping in mind post-high school plans. Departments concentrate on aligning courses across instructors and articulating between grades within the discipline. High school teachers also have the responsibility to prepare students for the "real world" because some students may stop formal education upon leaving grade 12 (or before); this accountability puts a heavy psychological burden on these educators, who also want their students to know the basic facts and concepts within their discipline. Additionally, although standards have existed throughout K–12 education, the stakes reach critical mass upon approaching graduation. Many schools now have graduation requirements and outcomes, which involve subject-specific and cross-curricular assessments, both in terms of standardized tests as well as portfolio development and authentic performances. Teachers who chose this level of education in the first place based their decision on a liking for teenagers and their own academic subjects. Thus, the newer emphases on reading, writing, and technology across the curriculum may seem like a "stretch" or a distraction for some traditionalists. Teachers may not have had in-depth training in these areas so may feel uncomfortable incorporating these skills. The same reluctance may arise when library media teachers talk about information literacy: "Another sidebar to teach!" some educators may say. Needless to say, high school faculty may feel overwhelmed by competing demands.

Within this environment, library media teachers can use the following approaches to foster partnerships:

- Translate information literacy standards into the language of each academic discipline, such as the scientific method or debate paradigm.

- Participate in cross-disciplinary task forces on reading, technology, and similar initiatives.

- Provide training on producing electronic portfolios.

- Coordinate technology special interest groups (SIGs) by tool, learning outcome, and so forth.

- Coordinate school videotaping or broadcasting services.

Of course, individual teachers or specific groups of teachers reflect different priorities and approaches. These factors come into play when establishing partnerships. For example, one teacher may be the powerhouse in the school but may be too overextended to partner meaningfully; a less-established but still responsible teacher might work more enthusiastically on the desired project. Some narrowly defined projects might call for very targeted partners, such as focusing on ways that seventh-grade science fair students can research more effectively; other projects may be open to a variety of groups or individuals, such as using presentation tools effectively. In identifying a potential teacher partner, library media teachers should consider looking for some of the following qualities, which can act as catalysts for collaboration (Liebert, 2000, p. 37):

Experience and competence

Leadership within the school, such as mentoring

Interest in and care for students and the school

Open-mindedness and a willingness to take educated risks

Eagerness to share ideas and resources

Effective communication skills

Groups reflecting these characteristics also tend to collaborate well. Such teachers are able to work from a stance of strength and self-confidence. Comfortable with themselves, they are not threatened by different ideas or new approaches. It should be noted, however, that a strong school library media teacher can also awaken such characteristics in burgeoning teachers; sometimes it just takes longer for people to open their inner "gifts."

Library media teachers should pay special attention to student teachers because these burgeoning professionals are their likely future partners. At this stage they combine the best of both worlds: the newest educational training and a critical openness to site-specific operations. They are willing to try new approaches and ask for constructive feedback. If student teachers experience positive mentoring from school library media teachers, they are more likely to expect that kind of collaboration when they are hired as credentialed teachers. Following are some ways in which to optimize interaction with student teachers:

- Meet with the student teacher to discuss not only the library media center's but also the student's own agenda. Read the university's student teacher handbook. Clarify roles and expectations.

- Make the student teacher comfortable. Demonstrate how the library media center can be a safe haven. Keep in regular contact.

- Have the student teacher observe existing good collaborations with teachers and students. Share library media center products for the school community: bibliographies, Web pages, databases, and so forth.

- Work with the site mentor teacher and university supervisor in critiquing the student teacher. Ideally, the library media teacher should act as a "critical friend" who does not affect the grading system but can provide useful feedback.

- Be willing to help student teachers with their own research projects or technology learning. Sometimes universities do not have the K–12 technology resources that student teachers must eventually use; school libraries can showcase realistic and forward-thinking incorporation of technology.

Support Staff

Like the school library media teacher, a number of other professionals provide specialized expertise—and may be overlooked or underutilized. Typical services include counseling, health care, reading, technology, and special education. These staff members work within structures that offer safety nets for schools. However, because they normally do not have prescheduled classes, these specialists depend on collaboration with, or at least referrals from, the rest of the school community. In addition, their expertise is itself specialized and not fully comprehended by their counterparts. Even reading or resource specialists might not realize the library media teacher's true value.

School library media teachers should learn more about the objectives and skills of these support faculty:

- Academic counselors might not know about some of the good financial aid electronic resources; their own documents can have a presence on the library media center Web page.

- The library media teacher can share bibliotherapeutic books with personal counselors. Together they can build the collection to help students deal with personal issues.

- Career counselors and library media teachers can develop a videotape collection about local community businesses and services.

- The school nurse and library media teacher can display and distribute materials on wellness. The media center can purchase medical reference works. Together the library media teacher and the nurse can create a database of local health services.

- The media center can provide audiobooks for children with special needs and work with the special education teacher to locate and incorporate appropriate software and assistive technology. Together they can show teachers how to accommodate learning differences and parents how to support their children's challenges.

- The library media teacher can share popular materials, including "hot" Web sites, with reading specialists to motivate students to read. Together they can help teachers and parents work with struggling readers.

- The library media teacher and technology specialist can model technology teamwork. The library media teacher can focus on curricular issues while the technologist can contribute operational savvy. Although the technology specialist may have more knowledge of vendors and help desks, the library media teacher can bring organizational skills to the table. Because both parties can have varying backgrounds, they need to check prior knowledge before making inaccurate assumptions (e.g., a tech specialist may be a mentor teacher, and the library media teacher may have started as a lab technician). In any case, they become part of the total teaching team, participating in the design and delivery of learning activities.

Administrators

Many studies identify administrative leadership as a key component of healthy school communities. The principal and his or colleagues set the tone for the school, clarifying the institutional mission and supporting its implementation. They truly act as educational CEOs, overseeing and coordinating the entire site operation. The task can be overwhelming, considering the demands of personnel within the constraints of available resources (e.g., facilities, budget, time, materials). Additionally, administrators answer to district mandates and community concerns. When societal pressures and legislation seem to make schools the saving grace of children, administrators can feel overwhelmed. Certainly, administrators must keep in constant contact with the entire school community; hopefully, they engage in effective partnerships as well. Particularly in these days of participatory government and shared leadership, administrators must keep current on organizational collaboration as well as individual needs.

Because library media teachers work with all students and staff, they are uniquely poised to partner with administrators. They can see academic and systematic patterns, so their participation in site councils and schoolwide initiatives can represent a broad-based perspective. Because the library media center cuts across grade levels and subject domains, library media teachers offer a less biased point of view and can see where duplicative efforts can be minimized. With their organizational skills, library media teachers can also develop schoolwide databases and Web sites that present institutional information for easy access.

In support of administrative functions, library media teachers can conduct research on reform issues and help administrators keep current on educational technology trends. They can also help administrators take advantage of publications, listservs, and other electronic tools, such as the National School Board Association's Web site (http://www.nsba.org). Furthermore, as the program administrative function of the media center becomes more evident, the school's administrators will accept library media teachers at the site's decision table. Together they can help support positive change in the school and community.

Ways in which library media teachers can partner with administrators in terms of technology include

- developing effective telecommunications mechanisms, such as an intranet or listservs, to facilitate staff communication;

- helping identify staff development needs through online surveys;

- providing Web tutorials on school issues;

- developing a videotape archive of best instructional practices;

- helping disaggregate data using statistical programs;

- comparing school data with other communities;

- researching funding sources; and

- coordinating knowledge management efforts.

Paraprofessional Staff

Schools could not carry out their missions without the help of paraprofessional staff. Be it the office secretary, building maintenance supervisor, cafeteria worker, or security officer, each person helps provide a safe and orderly environment for students and staff. Library media center paraprofessionals help build important links with these staff, particularly if they belong to the same union or are considered peers with these folks. The media center paraprofessional represents the media center's interests and can smooth the way for collaborative action in support of the center. The media center professional can also provide staff development opportunities or advocate for paraprofessional inclusion in school decision making. As library media center professionals and paraprofessionals work together as a team, they offer a consistent message about the media center and its potential. Examples of paraprofessional collaboration include

- developing and maintaining a list of toxic chemicals and healthy alternatives,

- collaboratively training on school administrative software systems,

- collecting and organizing educational policies and procedures,

- updating job descriptions,

- researching multicultural menus,

- evaluating wireless communication devices, and

- developing conflict-resolution training.

School Board

The school board acts as the policy-making body of the school or district; ultimately, its goal is to exploit community resources to ensure that all students can succeed. The National School Board Association (http://www.nsba.org) lists the following activities of school boards:

- Come to consensus about expectations for students.

- Establish standards aligned with external sources and share information about them.

- Determine how students can meet standards.

- Ensure multiple assessment means and track progress regularly.

- Align resources to objectives.

- Ensure a positive learning environment where all children learn and staff are supported.

- Collaborate with the political and business communities.

- Encourage continuing education and improved plans through analysis of data and community input.

Although school boards represent community interests, they should have a firm grasp of school issues to ensure student success through systemic support. In this picture, too often library media teachers appear before school boards only to request something for the library media center. This approach reinforces a parent-child relationship rather than a collegial partnership, as well as fostering a warped sense of the media center program. School library media teachers should identify and help meet board information needs; then they can help solve issues that come before the board as well as direct the actions of board members. Because school boards enjoy a tacit relationship with local government, they can encourage support of the library media center, so they are strong potential partners even beyond district borders.

In terms of technology, library media teachers should also look carefully at the technical expertise of school board members. Although it might be assumed that members might be less comfortable with technology because of age, some officers might well represent high-tech companies. In either case, the library media teacher can meet board members at their individual level, shaping partnerships accordingly. Strategies for forming these partnerships include

- attending board meetings, or at least reading board minutes, and helping to archive documents on the Internet to raise community awareness;

- researching board issues and helping to post findings;

- developing community databases and helping board members network with community constituents;

- training board members on advocacy methods and helping to promote school support; and

- facilitating discussions online among board members, school staff, and the larger community.

Students

Students constitute a powerful link with the community and can serve as influential partners. Even primary-aged children affect the community as they link family and school. Younger students mainly relate to their families, but by the time students reach middle school they have developed strong peer relationships. In high school students play a significant role in school governance as well as volunteering or working in the community.

Library media teachers see their job mainly in terms of helping students, and they often seek student help as aides. However, this approach reinforces a hierarchical relationship. Students can bring experiences and insights to the table that can inform library media teachers and help them improve the school community as a whole, specifically insights into how students think, new perspectives, peer teaching skills, and potential advocacy. The library media center can also benefit students by providing challenging training and responsibility, an arena in which to share expertise, practice for future work, and public recognition. A more balanced sense of the situation would acknowledge the adult role of the library media teacher but also foster leadership training for young people.

As do the other school community constituents, students need to be understood and respected. Students are usually perceptive about adult sincerity and caring. They also want fair treatment and resent condescending or sarcastic attitudes. They want to feel that the library media teacher is interested in them as unique individuals, not just as media center users. Despite some students' overt behaviors, they have tender egos and truly want acceptance by and approval from library media teachers and other adults. When students feel that they are equals as human beings, they will usually respond well and make good supportive partners.

The group identity of students must also be recognized and respected. Part of growing up is determining both personal identity and group affiliation; hence, students assume different roles in different surroundings. One of the library media center's strengths is its image as a safe and neutral place for students both individually and in groups. Library media teachers must be careful to acknowledge possible prejudices about groups (e.g., jocks, Goths, bimbos, slackers) and work hard to overcome those stereotypes to reach each student's contributions. On the other hand, if a student belongs to a group, the library media teacher can leverage that affiliation by asking that student to liaise with the others for possible collaborative efforts. Such efforts can result in graduation gifts to the library media center, sponsors and helpers for media center events, and underwriting of technology-related supplies.

Beyond the social and emotional considerations, library media teachers should plan carefully when working with students as partners. To start with, goals should be short and concrete so both parties can "test the partnership waters." Of course, the task should be meaningful for both the library media center and the students; dusting shelves is usually not a smart choice. Students should demonstrate that they know the skill to be used or should be trained as necessary. The library media teacher may ask a student to create a flyer only to find out that the student cannot type or do good layouts. Additionally, both parties need to feel comfortable enough with each other to negotiate changes, such as increased responsibility or a change in task; some students do not want a long-term commitment, or they may want to explore different aspects of the same project (e.g., reviewing Internet sites instead of maintaining Web pages). Library media teachers should continue to supervise and interact personably with students even when they can work independently; students want to feel wanted and appreciated—and may need that extra boost to keep them going or to encourage them to expand their contributions. Of course, recognition for good partnerships is vital, even if the project is small.

When adding technology into the student equation, library media teachers should not assume that all youth are tech-savvy. In fact, some student groups may pride themselves on their technology avoidance or may make fun of computer nerds. Others may fear technology. Library media teachers also should confront the Digital Divide directly and ensure that all students have equitable access to technology as needed. A number of Digital Divide issues exist, and library media teachers can address them in partnership with students:

Gender issues: Females now equal males in terms of their use of the Internet. Telecommunications, in particular, interest girls. Library media teachers should carefully consider acceptable use policies relative to e-mail and chats; when students abuse e-mail privileges or engage in possibly dangerous practices such as lewd conversations with over-age chatters, library media teachers may tend to limit telecommunications altogether. A more positive approach is to form a student committee to discuss these issues and develop fair guidelines. In other technology uses, girls may be under-represented. If a girls' club exists at school, the library media teacher might work with the members to help them improve their technology literacy and to ensure that the library media center provides software programs that meet girls' interests.

Language barriers: Library media center Web pages should include resources in languages representing the school population. Electronic translation programs should also be available on the opening screen. CD-ROMs such as *Rosetta Stone* should be acquired to help all students gain language skills. When coaching students, the library media teacher can enlist the help of bilingual students.

Literacy issues: Library media center Web pages should include easy-to-read resources and multimedia features as reading clues. Videotapes and audiobooks help students with reading problems; the library media teacher can encourage all types of students to suggest titles to be purchased in these formats. The library media center may also be "typecast" as a book place. To broaden the media center's reputation, the library media teacher can advise film appreciation or video clubs.

Socioeconomic issues: The library media teacher can promote equity through laptop borrowing and extended hours. Students who do not have access to computers at home may need extra training, which the library media teacher can provide through Internet clubs that welcome the neophyte. Students who need jobs to continue school can partner with the library media teacher to develop job hotlines. Students of under-represented ethnic groups may not see themselves in Internet resources. The library media teacher, in partnership with these students, can produce documents that address those needs, then broadcast them via the Internet. Library media teachers can help migrant students via the Internet.

Of course, those students who *are* technologically literate constitute very valuable partners in library media center services. They can

- evaluate technology resources such as hardware, software, and Internet documents;

- help acquire, install, and troubleshoot software and hardware;

- train and coach the school community in the use of technology;

- develop tutorials in the use of technology in various formats (Web, print guidesheets, audiocassettes, videotapes);

- create technology-based products such as databases, spreadsheets, multimedia, and Web pages;

- produce and edit videotapes; and

- advocate technology incorporation in the school community and specifically in the library media center.

Communications

A special set of school community groups worth cultivating is publishers or, more generally, communicators. At the school level, several media channels exist: student newspaper and yearbook, school Web pages, parent newsletter, and department or principal communications. Library media teachers can also produce publications, assuming the role of media channel. In working with school media, the library media teacher should establish good relationships with the editors and advisors. School editors change regularly, so the library media teacher should visit the school "news room" with every staff turnover to ensure continuity of connection. Positive and regular communication can prevent or minimize problems.

Media relationships require careful attention. In one case, a student editorial condemned the school library media center's extensive technical magazine collection, asserting that such in-depth coverage marginalized other subscriptions. In talking with the newspaper advisor, the library media teacher found out that students controlled content and authority, so she went to the writer and explained that all but one subscription was free because of her networking activity, and also showed the writer the online magazine collection. She also explained that she had advised student newspapers in the past, and talked with the student about verifying information—which had not been done in this case. The student retracted the story, and the student press wrote more accurately and positively about the media center subsequently. By taking the time to teach the student rather than write a condemning letter, that library media teacher cemented another partnership.

Case Studies

Tamalpais Union High School District (California) developed a technology aide program, which enables students to develop technology skills while helping the school community to use technology effectively. This program was designed by this author.

Erica Peto et al.'s *Tech Team* (1998) explains how middle schoolers can help the school community maintain technology resources. The book is based on Peto's school's team approach to student involvement.

In El Paso's Ysleta District, a literacy/biliteracy initiative led to several projects developed by middle school faculty: an after-school tutoring program, an ESL computer lab, extended library media center hours, and an Accelerated Reader program (Wood & Dickinson, 2000, p. 188).

Students at Horace Mann Academic Middle School (San Francisco), in partnership with Newcomer High School and Thurgood Marshall High School, developed the world's first student online Chinese magazine. The publication includes Chinese-language electronic software directions and a special coding program so readers can access it in their primary language (http://www.sfedfund.org/grants/lpd1999.html).

De Orillas A Orilla (From Shore to Shore) is an international telecommunications network linking teachers and students in the United States, Puerto Rico, Argentina, Canada, and Mexico. Team-teaching partnerships facilitate cross-cultural, collaborative student projects (http://www.orillas.org).

The Library of Congress's American Memory Fellows Program builds on teacher-librarian teams, which develop interactive student projects using digitized primary resources. Exemplary lessons are posted on LOC's Web page (http://lcweb2.loc.gov/ammem/ndlpedu/amfp).

The California School Library Association produces an annual newsletter of exemplary projects involving classroom and library media center-teacher collaboration, much of which incorporates technology. The publication also features leading administrators who partner successfully with library media teachers to help improve schools (http://www.schoolibrary.org).

Close Up

The handbook in this section is designed for teachers to help them work with parent volunteers. It is one part of a package of documents guiding a countywide coordinated program for K–12 schools.

Marin County Office of Education Volunteer Education Program Teacher Handbook

Introduction

Volunteers are an important part of the process of making education a meaningful experience for students at all grade levels. Although volunteers cannot substitute for professional expertise, they reflect and help implement the school's vision. By sharing time, skills, and knowledge, volunteers make a productive contribution to a child's education, as well as providing much needed support to classroom teachers who are entrusted with the responsibility of educating our future generations.

Some of the possible volunteer functions that volunteers assume include:

Tutor: reading, mathematics, library skills

Supervisor: playground, field trips, lunch

Programmer: planning and implementing school events and services

Communicator: making displays and posters, designing flyers and newsletters, "selling" the school, storytelling, acting as a liaison to the community

Producer: desktop publishing, videos, slide shows, displays, Web pages

Technician: operating, maintaining, troubleshooting, training others

Office assistant: processing, doing reception work, filing

Fund-raiser

Interviewing

The first encounter with a new volunteer is the most important, for it establishes the relationship between the two persons. Moreover, it paves the way for effective school utilization of volunteers. The first meeting should include the basics: the school's mission, an overview of the functions within the school, the role of the volunteer, role of the school staff and their relationship to the volunteer, and the specific contributions of the individual volunteer.

Volunteers should be interviewed in terms of their interests, abilities, and time commitments. Next, school duties should match their personal profiles; the job assignment should also take into consideration the volunteer's preference for one steady job or a variety of tasks. Ideally, each volunteer function should include a job description. Only after policies, clear expectations, and performance standards are stated should volunteers be trained.

Training

One main factor in good use of volunteers is effective training of them. When volunteers learn how to do a task well and contribute to the school through their service, they become positive ambassadors to the community. Time spent in explaining how to work in the school is a valuable investment.

Training is actually an ongoing activity paralleling the needs and interests of the volunteers as they grow in their role at school. Typically, the volunteer supervisor (e.g., classroom teacher) gives an overview of the job and trains for basic assistance. Additional training depends on the teacher's needs, volunteer capability and interest, and available time. Flexibility and good documentation (e.g., manuals and reference sheets) are key factors for successful small-group and individual training. In general, on-the-job training consists of these steps:

- The teacher explains and models the correct procedure.

- The teacher guides the volunteer step by step in the specific procedure.

- The teacher supervises the volunteer's work and corrects actions as needed.

- The volunteer carries out the process correctly and independently.

Sometimes the best training is not a formal presentation by the teacher, but a demonstration by a practicing volunteer or a clear guidesheet that a volunteer can use independently.

Since most volunteers are adults, their learning characteristics and needs must be taken into account.

- First, adults are experienced learners. Teachers should build on such expertise, going from the known to the unknown. Teacher and volunteer should have a reciprocal relationship.

- Adults have limited time. Training must be well-prepared and immediately useful.

- Adults learn in response to their own interests and needs. Teachers should foster self-improvement. The trainer should also consider physical needs: breaks and food.

- Adults have strong habits. They need to feel safe so they can take learning risks.

- Adults need to see results. They need to practice new skills, preferably with coaching.

What are the implications for training? Make it useful and meaningful, make it hands-on. Deal with mixed abilities and a variety of learning styles. Let volunteers share experiences. Make it fun!

Although most volunteer training is small-scale, considered thinking and planning will pay off in higher volunteer contribution. If training is done in a convincing and engaging manner, volunteers will respect the teacher and carry out the needed task with more conviction and efficiency. Each volunteer should record personal training sessions, and a central training spreadsheet should be maintained, with the session name on one axis and the volunteer's name on the other axis.

Development

Supervision can make or break the effective use of volunteers. A delicate balance exists between breathing down a volunteer's neck and abandoning the person. Because each volunteer has a different response to supervision, the teacher must be sensitive to each volunteer's needs and comfort zone. As the volunteer is learning a new skill, closer supervision is necessary to clarify details about the particular function. As the volunteer demonstrates competency, then supervision can assume a lighter touch. Volunteers recognize degrees of supervision and value autonomy because of the trust that it implies. Of course, the most positive situation is when the teacher and volunteer work side by side. The immediate supervisor should also oversee volunteer scheduling, evaluation, and problem solving; the volunteer coordinator takes a schoolwide perspective on these matters.

Sometimes a mentality may exist that volunteers are second-rate, that they cannot be dependable or accountable. Neither is true. Volunteers need to know that their contributions are meaningful, and that their performance levels are important. A name tag with the school logo is one symbol of a significant contribution. Most people want to do their best and may need help in knowing how to improve their performance. The sooner problems can be recognized and solved in cooperation with the volunteer, the more successful the experience will be for both parties.

Equally important is recognizing good work. Particularly when persons are not paid for their work, they need to know that they are valued, especially for specific tasks that are well done. A few ideas follow:

- Give at least token gifts for service: note pads, pins, certificates, student work.

- Throw a party.

- Write a personal thank-you note or a good reference letter.

- "Promote" them to more responsible work.

Volunteers not only give valuable service hours, they serve as supporters to get out the word in the community that the school deserves strong financial and moral support.

TEAMING WITH FAMILIES

8

Family involvement affects students—and schools—significantly. Even if parents never step on the school grounds, their roles as first teacher and life support contextualize student learning throughout the children's upbringing. Because of their intimate knowledge about children as well as their connections to the rest of the community, family partnerships should be carefully garnered and optimized. Schools with good parent partnerships outperform other schools, command greater respect in the community, and witness better teacher morale. On their part, by being involved in school matters, parents can learn skills to help their children as well as gain opportunities for self-improvement. Both families and schools heavily invest their time and effort in the cause of youth; they share responsibility for preparing students and influence them in both overt and subtle ways. As partners they can support and sustain each other in this mutual interest.

Levels of Involvement

Parental involvement in schools, and the school library media center specifically, varies largely, from none to daily professional work. Over the years, researchers (Epstein et al., 1997) have identified five major levels of parent involvement:

Family obligation: maintaining a healthy home environment for learning

Involvement at school: as a volunteer

Home education: monitoring student homework and communicating high expectations for student achievement at school

Decision making and advocacy at school: through governing bodies and associations

Community collaboration: as a liaison with the school and in support of child welfare.

School library media teachers can leverage each of these levels to promote the library media center and the school community as a whole. Moreover, technology can facilitate the following strategies:

Family obligation: Web-based documents and hyperlinks, as well as print publications, offer tips for reading areas, book and electronic purchases, and models of good reading habits.

Involvement at school: Parents can volunteer on a regular basis in the library media center, work on a special event, speak to classes, advise a media center tech club, organize Friends groups, or do behind-the-scenes work such as fund-raising or acquiring grants.

Home education: Library media teachers can hold workshops for parents about Internet use and can also produce videos to be broadcast on local community channels to guide parents in some of the following activities: reading and surfing the Internet with children, monitoring or limiting television and telephone use and helping children schedule homework time, and supervising childhood friends and staying involved in children's after-school activities.

Decision making at school: Library media teachers can do online research for parent groups. They can share criteria for selecting technology products and spearhead technology strategic plans with parental input. Library media teachers can train parent decision makers in advocacy skills and point them to media center-related associations that do advocacy work.

Community collaboration: Library media center databases can provide contact information about community resources; media center Web pages can link to these sources as well. Media center aides can help develop community-based Web pages and videotape community events that support reading and other media center values.

Many of the library media center's services affect the family. When parents receive a form to approve their child's Internet use, they see how the school expects the family to share responsibility in ethical behavior. Likewise, when parents are asked if their child may check out a laptop from the media center, they see the lengths to which the school is willing to go to ensure that all students have access to technology. And as library media teachers work with students each day, they can draw attention to links with the family. Indeed, as children talk with their families, they communicate their feelings about the media center. If the library media teacher goes the extra mile, that support may be mentioned around the dinner table—and if he or she is rude, that too will get communicated. The more that the library media teacher involves students on an individual basis and gives them leadership roles such as Web designer or Internet reviewer, the more likely it is that families will hear about those activities and will be willing to support the library media teacher and get involved themselves.

Factors in Parent Partnerships

Parents usually want the best for their children, but they may not get involved actively in education. Several factors affect the likelihood of establishing a partnership and maintaining it. The more quickly library media teachers recognize the following issues and address them, the better will be the results:

Low expectations: Parents may have low expectations of schools, their children, and themselves. Usually the best way to counter those feelings is to provide positive models: good sample student work, examples of parent involvement, testimonials about personal growth of students and parents. Indeed, parents need not agree with a teacher about education, but the two parties *do* need to agree that each child is important and deserves the best education. Parents need to feel respected—and listened to.

Personal issues: Parents may not be interested in becoming involved or may fear the unknown. They may not be experienced and so not feel that they can contribute. Again, when existing partners share their stories, be it at a PTA meeting or through newsletters, potential partners can identify with these successes. Cultural factors may limit parent participation. Schools also must be sensitive to various family or traditional values and find ways for parents to help without risking cultural conflicts. For example, some women might need to stay home, but they could do artwork for school or babysit for other parent volunteers. Parents also need to feel assured that the school will train them for whatever task must be accomplished. On the other hand, some parents may feel overqualified; schools should interview potential partners carefully to find the right "fit."

Family issues: Particularly as children get older, they might not want to have their parents at school, or parents might not think that they have much influence on their children's lives. In other cases, children might need to make money or help supervise siblings because of parents' working hours. Parents should know that they can get involved behind the scenes as well as in the front office. They also should understand how subtle details in education can make a difference. A parent can feel powerful knowing that he or she might be touching the lives of *other* parents' students.

Logistics: Even with the best intentions, parents may run into problems that limit or constrain their involvement. They may have small children to supervise; schools might have names of people who can babysit while the parent is helping. They may have transportation issues, which the school might be able to address through carpooling or by crafting a task that can be done at home. Parents might need a home computer but not have the money for one; schools should find other partners, such as businesses, who can donate such equipment. Language or reading barriers might exist; again, parent "buddies" can help translate—and coach that problematic parent. In other cases, school policies can block involvement, so those rules may have to be reviewed or even modified as deemed appropriate. For example, hours of campus access might be "bent" to accommodate special tasks such as cable setup.

Schools should provide a safe and welcoming atmosphere for families as well as for their children, a sense of community. And schools also must reach out to parents where *they* live. One way to get parents involved is to identify those centers in the community where parents tend to congregate or feel comfortable: a religious institution, a community center, a sports arena. Schools can connect to those institutions through meetings, publications, and Internet links. In the final analysis, space is not the key factor; rather, good leadership and communication are. Teachers and other school personnel often need training in ways to communicate and work closely with parents. They should clarify for themselves what roles parents play in education and then communicate those roles clearly to parents. When the entire school works together for the benefit of all children, parents are more likely to believe in that vision and want to be a part of the effort.

Technology's Role

Technology plays a significant role in parent partnerships, as both an obstacle and a facilitator. Some parents fear computers or have little experience with them. Library media teachers should make sure that information is always available in print form as well as electronic form. They may also have to "hold hands" with wary parents who need to use an automated catalog to find desired materials. With a willing and patient spirit, though, library media teachers can actually help parents feel more comfortable with such equipment. A good example is Internet use. Some parents worry about pornographic or other inappropriate Web sites that their children may encounter. The library media teacher can offer a workshop on family use of the Internet, showing parents how they can find good educational material and be able to evaluate sources critically. If a parent volunteer is used to a typewriter, the library media teacher can ease that person onto a word processor and demonstrate the editing benefits of the technology.

For those folks who use technology regularly, the library media center can gain credibility if its technology is current—and may get needed support if it lags behind technologically. Tech-savvy parents can install software and troubleshoot hardware. Certainly, the word processor expert or spreadsheet authority can offer welcome relief to an overworked library media teacher or a frustrated student. Parents might also lend a hand in Web page design or hosting. Parents in business, particularly in technology, may donate valuable resources; some companies such as IBM have programs through which parents pay matching funds so a computer can be donated to a library media center. In terms of strategic planning for technology, expert parents provide valuable insights and human network connections.

Throughout the process of establishing and maintaining parent partnerships, technology comes in handy:

- *Recruitment* may be done via Web page, broadcast video, or local listserv. Libraries can print and distribute a series of flyers about specific ways to get involved.

- *Volunteer applications and interviews* may be done online.

- *Goal setting* can be facilitated through concept-mapping software and online surveys. Parents at a distance can discuss in real time as a group using chat software.

- *Training* can incorporate videotape, multimedia, and Web tutorials.

- *Job placement* and development can use databases to check off skills and match tasks appropriately.

- *Scheduling* is facilitated through groupware or online calendaring.

- *Off-site tasks* for the library media center can be done using home computer systems, especially if they can connect via telecommunications to school. Groupware editing of documents enables all partners to track each other's contributions and responses.

- *Ongoing communication* is enhanced through voice-mail, listservs, and other Internet services. Library media center Web pages can include translation services to help non-English-speaking families keep current about school matters. FamilyEducation.com offers free Web-based e-mail for schools. Students can download their computer work onto videotape for parents to view with VCRs (more prevalent than home computers).

- *Evaluation* is enhanced through online discussion. Productions and events can be videotaped to facilitate detailed analysis.

- *Recognition* looks professional with computer-generated certificates. Digital cameras facilitate capturing volunteer moments that can be imported into presentations and Web pages (with permission).

The Virtual Volunteer

In the age of technology, volunteer work can be done off-site and online. Volunteers can design and maintain school/community databases, Web pages, and interactive discussion or tutoring groups. They can produce professional-looking documents and other products. They can orient, train, mentor, and translate—in short, provide valuable services to people who otherwise might not get involved with education. In addition, they can play a strong advocacy role through online links to other groups.

People who want to be "virtual" volunteers (VV) tend to be tech-savvy and task-oriented. They may have difficulty getting to school or scheduling their time around school clocks. They may not like bureaucratic systems or enjoy face-to-face meetings; "Give me the job and the support, and get out of my way" might be a fitting mantra for VVs. Individuals who are likely VV candidates have the technical expertise and resources to do the work and communicate effectively with the school. They should be dependable self-starters who recognize and meet deadlines. They should also document their work, follow school guidelines, and practice ethical behaviors (e.g., not take advantage of their volunteer role to spread confidential information).

How do schools recruit these potentially valuable partners? Obviously, the first approach is to ask students' parents through existing structures such as registration and PTA groups. The school's Web page can include volunteer listings; an interactive volunteer form models a technology-friendly environment and acts as a self-screening filter. It also makes sense to link with other community members by reaching out to techie natural "habitats": the Internet and local technology groups. Many communities have technology newspapers or Web sites that list user groups and note community projects. Microsoft has a volunteer kiosk as part of its site builder network (http://www.guidestar.org/classifieds/ms_ sbn.adp). Two useful Web sites for general recruitment are http://volunteermatch. org and http://serviceleader.org/vv/index.html. The former is a user-friendly service that enables users to find opportunities by location or type of service and permits nonprofit organizations to register and post volunteer opportunities. (*Note:* Schools should not post volunteer openings until tasks are firmly identified and support systems are in place; getting a pool of applicants without assigning them a job will backfire, making it more difficult in the future to get volunteers.) Serviceleader.org, operating out of the University of Texas at Austin, supports the Virtual Volunteering Project. It acts as a clearinghouse of resources for agencies and volunteers. Ellis and Craven's (2000) *Virtual Volunteering Guidebook,* which can be downloaded from that site, provides valuable details on how to manage VVs.

As with other volunteers, schools need to interview and negotiate with potential VVs. The school volunteer liaison, be it a coordinator or the specific person with whom the volunteer will collaborate, should meet the VV in person, even if it means going off-campus. A neutral, safe location convenient to the VV, such as a public library, is a professional and level playing field. The following points should be covered during the interview:

> Potential task and products—and context within the school
>
> Necessary skills and responsibilities
>
> Time frame and other project parameters
>
> Procedures and communication requirements
>
> Resources and support, including training

Agreements should be written, and supporting documents (e.g., letters of recommendation, confidentiality policies, etc.) should be filed for future reference. As with other volunteers, every care must be taken to ensure that students and staff will be safe with this volunteer. A good idea is to "pilot-test" the volunteer by giving him or her a short-term, concrete task and evaluating its outcome. As mutual trust builds, so too can responsibility.

The school liaison should set a professional tone and keep in touch with the VVs, training them as needed, monitoring their work, redirecting them as necessary, and publicly recognizing their achievements. Even though virtual volunteers may not set foot on the school grounds, they need to feel included in school matters and know that their contributions help students.

Case Studies

Libraries work with local agencies to facilitate and support parent involvement. An agency van can provide free transportation, daycare services can provide babysitting help, several agencies offer parenting classes, and public housing can provide a computer for volunteer use.

Substance abuse is a major problem in many communities. Students and parent volunteers can create discussion videotapes about this issue and broadcast them on community channels. The library media center can lend the equipment, train the production staff, and circulate archived copies of the tapes.

San Francisco's main Spanish-language television station sponsored a series of public service announcements and news coverage to foster education among Latino families. The initiative, called Exito Escolar, also helps families understand the educational system.

Library media center Web pages can contain links to full-text periodicals and reference materials so families can access them at home for their own education. These Web pages should also include information targeted to parents: parenting skills, filtering issues, job hotlines, health information, and community resources. School library media center Web pages provide needed outreach to home-schooled and migrant children. Parenting pages can really help teen parents who might be embarrassed to ask for information in school.

Libraries for the Future has established a network of Family Place libraries that provide resources and services for early education and family support. These community centers are staffed by outreach library media teachers who develop programs for both children and parents and offer access to electronic resources that foster reading readiness and parent education. A similar program, Community Technology Centers, trains communities in information technology and career preparation skills. These two efforts follow the principle of meeting families where they live rather than making them come to the school to learn or get involved.

Libraries can develop activity kits for parents to check out and use at home with their children. These kits can include audiotapes, videotapes, and CD-ROMs, along with guides for their use.

Literacy is a family issue. Libraries can circulate videotapes and provide Web links to help parents read with their children and also improve their own literacy skills.

Microsoft helps families get excited about technology through its Family Technology Night program. School library media centers can sponsor these free events and use this opportunity to showcase their own technology resources and services.

The Children's Partnership, in collaboration with the National PTA and the National Urban League, has developed *The Parents' Guide to the Information Superhighway: Rules & Tools for Families Online* (Children's Partnership, 1998). Free copies are available to school libraries, which can use them in conjunction with family workshops on Internet use.

Parents at Corona Avenue Elementary School (California) have little access to computers at school. However, the school gave them computer-use workshops, and "graduates" now teach computer classes for other parents and their children. They also have a parent link on the school Web page (http://www.corona.bell.k12.ca.us) where they post information about their classes and links to technology sources.

Library media centers can involve grandparents as storytellers and readers. Grandparents also make substantial donations to help their grandchildren. Students can interview grandparents and capture their memories on audio- or videotape.

The American Library Association (ALA) has several resources for parents about technology: educational Web sites, multimedia tutorials, and online homework help (http://www.ala.org). School library media teachers can use these resources as well as volunteer for KidsConnect online homework help. Alternatively, local school library media teachers could develop their own homework hotlines on the Internet. ALA offers ongoing advocacy training, including workshops for leaders to emulate on the local level; school library media teachers can train parents in these skills, both to advocate for youth as well as to support libraries.

Close Up

Marin County collaborated with a site library media center media teacher, site technology specialist, agency volunteer service expert, and local parents to develop a series of training modules to involve parents and other community members in meaningful ways in public schools.

Library Volunteer Orientation

Learning Objectives

By the end of the session the volunteers will be able to

- describe the role of the volunteer within the library setting,

- explain library policy and procedures regarding volunteer work,

- identify basic library operations,

- define basic library terms,

- describe staff and student relationships, and

- list at least five skills to help students become independent learners.

Training Resources

Library volunteer guide

Flip chart/newsprint or chalkboard

Pencils, pens, coloring tools

Handouts on library terms and DDC

Optional: overhead projector, VCR

Trainer Notes

- Use experiential learning cycle: experience > share > process > generalize > apply. ALWAYS PROCESS!

- For a large group reporting out, ask for sample responses.

- Consider having an assistant to act as a recorder/go-fer.

- Don't force anyone to participate.

- Provide "stretch" break.

Table: Training Outline

Time	Objective	Strategies
pre	Make volunteers comfortable	Show school video, photos; do cross-word
5	Introduce training agenda	Presentation
10	Know volunteer commitment	Peer interview on reasons for library volunteering; discuss volunteer benefits and characteristics
15	Describe library operations	Presentation/Q&A about libraries
10	Define basic library terms	Complete and discuss library terms puzzle
10	ID volunteer role within library	Create chart with headings: librarian/teacher/volunteer; list tasks for each (filing, tutoring, etc.)
15	Describe staff/student relationships	Brainstorm possible problems working with others; each small group solves one problem
15	List skills to foster independence	Role-play dependent/independent learning relationships
5 ID next steps	Generate library questions	
15	Understand library arrangement	Presentation on DCC and filing
5	Summarize/evaluate session	Share learning; evaluate learning; ask next questions

- Explain library policy and procedures regarding volunteer work.

- Identify basic library operations.

- Define basic library terms.

- Describe staff and student relationships.

- List at least five skills to help students become independent learners.

TEAMING WITH INSTITUTES OF HIGHER LEARNING

Too often institutions of higher education (IHE) are considered ivory towers of learning. During the 1999 American Library Association (ALA) Commission on Professional Education meetings, perceptions expressed revealed a disconnection between library media center schools and K–12 education. This situation is surprising, disconcerting—and unnecessary. Library media teachers need to understand how this view has come into being so they can develop strategies to not only overcome apparent obstacles but also leverage partnerships.

How IHEs Work

One of the keys to unlocking the secrets of universities is to understand the RTP process: retention, tenure, and promotion. This process determines which faculty are retained, nurtured, and recognized. The process is extended to hiring procedures as well.

The major areas of faculty assessment are teaching, scholarly and creative activity, and service. Institutions may weight these factors differently, but almost all will ask for evidence of quality work across the board. Hiring committees, which usually include faculty peers, department chairs, and a college representative, also look for faculty who match the school's philosophy and personality.

Now how does this translate into school connections? IHE's first priority is to meet institutional needs. Credential preparation programs are given highest priority in education programs. Professional development after issuance of the first credential is usually through extension services and is considered a self-sustaining effort with looser ties to the principal program.

Because undergraduate programs are typically assessed in terms of their cost-effectiveness, graduate programs sometimes have to justify their lower faculty-student ratio and other overhead costs more rigorously—and thus have to show more evidence of return for the institution's investment. Colleges of education with options for librarianship are the natural first choices of school library media teachers, although other colleges have potential. Both teacher and library media teacher credential programs tend to exist as post-baccalaureate options.

Teaching in Community

This teaching emphasis can play out well for school libraries. One of the recent trends in education, in counterpoint to K–12 teaching, is *service learning*. Usually this term refers to the practice of presenting theories and principles that students then apply in the community, hopefully providing service at the same time. Students reflect on their experiences, generalizing their insights to reach a more profound level of understanding. Credential programs welcome the opportunity to visit school sites. Obviously, those sites with richer and more varied resources and instruction offer attractive models. Schools benefit from this experience in two ways: Their programs show progress and thus become more attractive to the community and other grant-givers, and their schools are exposed to the newest educational theories to optimize student learning.

On the other hand, underdeveloped schools offer a seedbed for improvement. If the school is eligible for Title IV funding, colleges can work with them to provide needed resources through grant opportunities or equipment upgrades. If K–12 students are underperforming, credential candidates might use these sites to test interventions to help at-risk children.

Technology facilitates such interventions in several ways. Some students do not achieve because they read poorly due to language or learning style barriers. Learning aids such as multimedia presentations or Intellikey templates facilitate student learning by providing more contextual cues for reading comprehension. Because classroom teachers are so busy, they welcome these products that make their tasks less labor-intensive. What the practitioner offers is skill in child diagnosis, which helps the college student shape the learning aide to fit student needs.

Technology also assists communication, so college and K–12 personnel can discuss educational issues via e-mail or online chats. The communication can be as easy as the teacher or library media teacher making a brief note about an immediate crisis and then sending the information at the end of the day to the university, thus providing excellent case study material for discussion. Telecommunications also help dialogue between collegiate and K–12 students. Two simple structures offer sample ways to further student interaction. A college student can be paired with a youngster, and they can converse online as the need arises, or when it is convenient for both parties. Because prompt, specific feedback is a key to learning, this mode of interaction is both efficient and confidential. A help desk manned by a college aide can also be established so youngsters can ask for online assistance. Not only do children learn how to pose questions and get individualized help, but the college students discover children's academic needs, and they can craft ways to meet those needs. The natural extension of such interaction is a student teacher internship, or the more generic term "field experience."

IHEs are constantly on the lookout for effective placements. As the International Society for Technology in Education (ISTE) technology standards are being put into place for K–12 students as well as for teachers, colleges must identify sites with the technological resources available to enable incoming teachers and library media teachers to observe and use technology-infused education. Schools with brand new equipment may well appreciate the instructional help that new educators can bring. As current education courses incorporate instructional design into their content, credential candidates can use those new skills in practical settings. As they partner with lead teachers, they can learn pedagogical techniques, transferring them into technology-infused lessons. Veteran teachers can try the new technologies for immediate academic impact.

The school library media center can play a leading role in the teaching students' field experiences by providing resources and expertise—or willingness to learn. In some cases, the library media teacher acts as the educational technology consultant for the candidates, sharing how resource-based learning can optimize student engagement. In this manner, the library media center significantly helps future teachers achieve. Laying the groundwork for teacher collaboration and infusion of technology will help all parties—and if a district hires the credential candidates, the benefits can be immediate.

With technology initiatives appearing on the scene, funding opportunities from local, state, and federal sources have also grown. Part of successfully obtaining such funding depends on broad-based planning, with community involvement. Both for school districts and the IHEs, coordination with their counterparts may be crucial.

For example, the issue of teacher competence has fostered a number of state and federal initiatives. The argument goes like this:

> **Question:** How can student achievement improve?
>
> **Answer:** Through technology.
>
> **Question:** How can technology be used effectively?
>
> **Answer:** Through trained teachers.
>
> **Question:** How can teachers be better trained?
>
> **Answer:** Through technology-competent faculty in teacher-preparation programs.

To achieve a sequence of education that transitions easily from freshman year to field experience, teacher preparation faculty must ensure that their candidates experience technology throughout their coursework, including field experience. Funding provides the means to hire adjunct educational technology specialists, who are often successful classroom or library media center teachers, to help college faculty infuse their curriculum with technology. These same folks can be the source of field experience placements. Because these experts teach content and techniques to college faculty, teacher/library media teacher candidates will experience consistent uses of technology, which will form the basis for their own professional practice.

This "seeding" from K–12 settings helps ameliorate the disconnection that sometimes happens when faculty do not visit schools in action. Not only can practitioners bring insights and sample student work to the campus, but college faculty might be more apt to see how their adjunct experts practice in the field. Another interesting approach is videotaping such sessions. In some cases, the colleges have videotaping services; in other situations, K–12 students do this. The resultant tapes can be used as pre- or in-service case studies, both at the college and at the district level. (With their knowledge of copyright issues, library media teachers can also ensure that necessary permissions are obtained.)

Professional Development

School library media teachers and other members of the community may wonder why universities do not offer more continuing education opportunities. The fact is, non-matriculated students (those people who are not enrolled in a degree or credential program) usually do not "count" when calculating the number of students. Professional development opportunities are usually run by extension services within the university, and the enrollment does not figure into the full-time equivalent student number that determines faculty load. In other words, college faculty are truly giving of themselves when they teach continuing education courses. Even if practicing school library media teachers attend "regular" classes to update their knowledge, they are considered extension students and do not add to the faculty load "coffers." Thus, continuing education workshops and their ilk become part of a faculty member's *service* record: contributing to the community. And that aspect of faculty life often does not count as much as programmatic instruction or research.

When continuing education opportunities do arise, school library media teachers should take advantage of them—and write encouraging letters of support, which faculty can use as "evidence" of their impact. School library media teachers can also finger likely peer "wannabes" (i.e., library paraprofessionals and classroom teachers who hunger to become real library media teachers) to attend these workshops as entrees into a formal credential or degree program.

School library media teachers might also be called upon by college faculty to share their experience with teacher/library media teacher candidates during courses. In a way, the practitioner experiences the same situations as the workshop faculty: more work and little professional recompense. However, these opportunities help everyone involved. School library media teachers garner more respect from their positive association with IHEs. The college strengthens its connections with the community and attracts more students through word-of-mouth. Students experience good models of school librarianship, which raises their expectations when out in the field—in support of high-quality school libraries and library media teachers. The concept of educational partnerships is concretized for easier transfer of learning into professional practice.

The partnerships for professional development have one more benefit: recruitment. If youngsters see positive relations among school library media teachers, educational candidates, and colleges, they may consider joining the profession themselves. It's one thing to see the same face day after day in the school media center, and another thing to see eager young near-professionals honing their skills in school settings. With the library field trying to recruit a diverse population, it can only help for youngsters to see themselves in the candidate pool; they might think that librarianship could be an open and inviting career opportunity.

Research Partnerships

One area of faculty work that is valued and rewarded is research and other scholarly activities. In this arena, school library media teachers and IHEs can help each other tremendously. Teacher and library media center faculty must be on the cutting edge of professional theory and principles. To a large extent, those abstractions arise from analyzing practice or are tested through observation in practical situations. In either case, school libraries provide the perfect setting for study.

On the most elementary basis, school library media teachers can help the profession by participating in research surveys. College faculty must collect data and describe education's reality to improve it. So although it takes time, completing surveys supports advancements in the profession. School libraries are often the communications link for teacher/library media center preparation faculty, so their goodwill is appreciated. The more school library media teachers can facilitate cooperation between their own staff and the student body, the more they can reap the benefit of research. For example, the American Association of School Librarians (AASL) is sponsoring research on reading habits as it tries to implement *Information Power.* By identifying critical factors that distinguish good readers, for example, library media researchers can develop interventions that have the potential to help less successful readers. In 2001, twenty states are involved in this research project and need the cooperation of schools at each level: elementary, middle, and high school. Statistics will be more valid when substantial numbers participate from around the country.

On another level, school library media centers can partner with library school faculty and graduate library candidates in small research projects. Master's degree candidates in particular usually must conduct some kind of applied research project or write a thesis paper. They might build upon existing research and use schools as sites to test the reliability of previous research findings or expand upon others' work. Alternatively, candidates might wish to explore original research questions. In some cases, candidates might not know what kinds of research are needed in the field, so school library media teachers can actually help shape the direction of research. Because school library media teachers might not have a strong research background themselves, or the resources and time to pursue research agendas, connecting to a local school librarian preparation program can prove a godsend for practicing school library media teachers. For example, a school may find that boys perform less well than girls in standardized reading tests. The local IHE could help analyze the problem and suggest helpful interventions. The university gains creditability, the school gets professional help to improve student achievement, and the profession itself advances in its theories and principles.

One avenue that the practicing school library media teacher might consider is "action research." This applied research model is based on a systematic cycle of inquiry. The library media teacher examines the environment and starts asking critical questions. "Hmm, I notice that students do not use magazines in their research projects; I wonder why?" The library media teacher identifies what kind of data are needed to answer the question, then collects and analyzes the information. "Well, the library media center has a good magazine collection, and I show students how to use magazine indexes, but students say they prefer to use the Internet." The library media teacher might need to dig deeper. How insightful are the student' research reports? How satisfied are teachers with the results? It might surface that the students do not realize the extent of the magazine collection; perhaps students need to find information within the last month before print indexes are published. The findings will dictate the needed intervention: either opportunities for students to examine the broad range of periodicals in the first place, or a need to subscribe to an online magazine index service to help students find immediate sources. After the intervention, or change in practice, is tested and results are analyzed, the library media teacher can determine its success—usually in terms of student learning. Action research does not try to control for all variables in the way that an empirical study might, but it does offer a first step toward systematic analysis and improvement of practice.

IHEs can facilitate the practitioner's action research. They can help with designing the study, identifying valid measurement instruments, collecting data, analyzing findings, and recommending effective strategies. Graduate students might well be available to provide research and technical assistance. Staff and students might provide consulting service to jump-start the process and garner schoolwide support. Usually, IHEs have research collections, including theses and dissertations that might provide clues for library studies. If a school library media teacher really becomes interested in research design, related courses are usually available through extension services. Why would IHEs be interested in helping? Action research provides another venue for student service learning—and offers data upon which to build professional theories.

Case Studies

Universities work in K–12 settings to provide teacher candidates with placements where technology incorporation is taking place. Universities also help teachers meet new professional technology standards.

Universities provide Web-based resources that students and families can access from home. They also partner with communities to provide technology instruction to increase family involvement in children's education and to ensure that migrant students can access teachers.

University libraries serve high school populations and work with feeder schools on curriculum articulation and collaborative collection development.

High school library media teachers serve as community college reference librarians and help design orientations for upper class students.

Library media teacher candidates assess local school libraries and develop improvement plans in conjunction with school personnel.

Close Up

This project between high school and college librarians facilitated bibliographic instruction for students and articulated library instruction between academic levels. The principal investigators in this project were the author and Harriet Talan of San Francisco State University.

Developing a Multimedia Library Skills Electronic Workbook

This project intends to develop a self-contained library skills "electronic workbook" that can be used by all types of libraries. The workbook consists of a core of units that teach basic information literacy skills, including how to use electronic resources, and supporting documents that help librarians administer and modify the workbook. This project will meet the documented need to teach basic information literacy skills to a large number of library users at a time of both increasing budget constraints and demands upon professional personnel.

Activities of the project include a) integrating computer-assisted information literacy skills units, which have been developed in the first phase of the project, into an "electronic workbook"; b) developing variations of the "electronic workbook" targeted to three different audiences: post-secondary school library users, public library users, and secondary school students; c) developing supporting printed materials to guide librarians on how to administer and customize the workbook to meet the needs of specific populations of library users; and d) testing and evaluating the materials to ensure that the electronic skills kit is effective and can be used by those who administer it in a completely self-sufficient manner.

This project will benefit all libraries and library users. Represented in California are the California State University libraries, a special library, school libraries, community college libraries, and public libraries. It has commitment from over 50 librarians at 40 libraries.

This project continues the federal grant "Teaching core library skills through multimedia." Other support for the first phase of the project came through a U. S. Department of Education grant and an Apple Library of Tomorrow award. In-kind support and facilities for development and testing are being provided by university and other libraries. Activities completed during the first phase of the project include design and evaluation of computer-assisted tutorials, drafting of evaluation and testing procedures, identification of evaluation sties, and dissemination and presentation of tutorials in progress.

Principles of human interface and computer-assisted instructional design are applied to achieve an interactive product. The software chosen can be adapted for local use by all types of libraries on both platforms (Mac and PC) and provides the flexibility to make it possible for the workbook to be used in a variety of settings, including classrooms, homes, media centers, and computer labs.

TEAMING
WITH
LIBRARIES

10

School library media teachers have a natural ally in other librarians that they don't always optimize. Behind their reluctance is the tension between librarianship and education. Although all librarians are educators to some degree, school library media teachers sometimes see themselves as teachers first—and prioritize their associations accordingly. Yet, no matter the setting, all librarians share the core professional values of collection development and retrieval. When they leverage their individual niches and complement each other's strengths, they can accomplish a great deal toward realizing the concepts of the learning community.

Building on Strengths

As each type of library brings to the table its strengths, it can allocate resources in a cost-effective manner to help all students succeed. For example, school library media teachers know students and curriculum in depth. They serve as educational partners, helping students become lifelong learners by teaching them research strategies and promoting teaching appreciation. School library media teachers also act as educational conduits as they work daily with teachers to craft learning experiences that meld concepts with relevant resources. And working with youth all day, school library media teachers understand learning developmental issues.

For their part, public librarians bring a broad perspective on resources and helping services. Because they serve all ages, they can help in articulating library assistance, particularly on a one-to-one basis. They also tend to hold more public programs and events, so they know how to plan with other community members effectively. Public librarians have the advantage of providing more neutral areas for library research; they have no passes and hold no sway in grading. (And they tend to have fewer discipline problems because students go to the public library basically because they want to rather than because their teachers made them.) Public libraries' extended hours also respond more realistically to student demands, especially those of teenagers.

Public libraries provide the core library services of the community. In hard times, when school library media teachers are laid off, public libraries usually remain to give basic service. In this scenario, their broad collections and user base provide them with support leverage; even if their staffing, hours, and budget are cut dramatically, they are rarely snuffed out completely. School library media teachers would do well to support these services in bad times, because public libraries bear the brunt of school library media center cutbacks.

Other types of libraries also play a role in school communities. Special libraries provide in-depth collections and services to a select population, such as medical professionals or lawyers. Higher education libraries also provide rich collections, usually heavy in research, to support ongoing scholarship, and they often allow high school students access, thus facilitating the transition from K–12 to college education. When advanced research projects are assigned in high schools, school library media teachers can serve as facilitators between students and faculty and these focused libraries to enable access to hard-to-find resources.

Traditional Partnerships

The heart of collaboration is communication. Librarians can tell each other about their own efforts and the influence of their constituents, be they local government or school initiatives. Certainly, because libraries are basically local entities, they are influenced by community issues. Typical events such as public library programs and teacher assignments affect library counterparts, and timely notice about them helps staff prepare to assist as needed. On a psychological level, school library media teachers may be able to help other types of librarians deal more effectively with students.

Collection development is a natural collaborative effort, as school and public libraries try to complement resources; usually schools reflect curriculum demands, and public libraries can provide more leisure reading. School library media teachers may also play an active role in suggesting titles and activities for public library summer reading programs. Local databases may be developed collaboratively, and displays can also be exhibited and coordinated across sites. On a more active professional level, school library media teachers sometimes substitute in public libraries after hours, and local librarians may serve on school communities. Librarians in different settings may join forces for library campaigns and community bond issues. Joint library volunteer programs may also be developed, both for youth and adults. In addition, staff development opportunities can cross library lines.

In each case, librarians carry out the following steps for forming partnerships:

- Identify mutual goals.

- Identify core personnel and resources.

- Negotiate roles and responsibilities.

- Train and support each other.

- Communicate processes and products between groups and reach out to the community.

- Evaluate efforts and modify them accordingly.

Service Through Technology

Partnering using electronic communication is a good way to start taking advantage of technology to help provide service. Local librarian groups can set up listservs or simple e-mail address books to ratchet up communication and solve library media center problems. As school library media teachers get teacher assignments e-mailed to them, they can forward those messages to the local public library. New book lists and system announcements can also be sent automatically or put on a Web page for quick perusal.

The greater community can participate in book discussion through inputting "testimonials" on public access catalog sections or interactive Web pages to be integrated into databases or Web sites. Libraries can jointly sponsor online "chats" about books and archive the discussions for their Web sites. In the past students have created audiotapes of booktalks, and public libraries have offered "dial-a-story" services via voice mail. Students can also videotape booktalks and air them on local cable stations or have them archived at school and public libraries with VCR access.

Interlibrary loan is a traditional service that greatly benefits from technology. At its most basic level, an ALA interlibrary loan form template can be created and stored for easy online access to speed up patron requests. The North Bay Cooperative Library System (NBCLS) used the Web platform to mount a multitype library union catalog, SuperSearch, that allowed patrons to reserve materials anywhere in the system and have them delivered to the library of their choice (http://www.nbcls.org). Of course, this service's success does not rely just on technology but also on the human coordination involved in reconciling loan periods, circulation policies, and fines.

Web pages constitute a major collaboration opportunity as well as a means to provide 24/7 service. Libraries of different types can create an umbrella Web page, with links to individual institutions. Such a product was created by the Greater Bay Areas Library Council, primarily for librarian use, and then extended to the local public (http://www.gbalc.org). The Greater Bay Area Library Council represents the body of librarians and library systems within the fourteen Greater Bay Area counties, from Mendocino to Monterey and from San Mateo to Contra Costa. The purpose of GBALC is to promote its members through collaborative communications, programs, and events. Regional projects, such as fax-based document delivery and Internet train-the-trainer workshops, were advertised and facilitated online. Later, the Web page included a directory of participating libraries so the public could type in a city or ZIP code and find information about their closest libraries. Search engines can be robust enough so patrons can locate libraries with specific collections. Web pages routinely include indexed Web site links; taking advantage of partnerships, each institution can focus on finding relevant Web sites in its area of expertise and contribute them to the overall effort by developing a template and protocol across libraries.

Online reference service can also be conducted collaboratively. Using an electronic expert system that matches the request to a particular library's collection emphasis, a patron can e-mail a reference question using an interactive Web form and receive a timely answer.

Beyond access to catalogs and information online, libraries are starting to collaborate on digitizing their collections. The leading institutions are currently academic libraries, such as the University of Virginia and the University of California at Berkeley. However, they are getting grants to foster collaboration with school libraries and historical societies to gather local unique documents and artifacts and archive them digitally so the public can have access to them freely.

Libraries are also venturing into the publication arena, particularly of local resources. Traditionally, libraries have collected local documents (e.g., newspaper clippings, programs, photographs, town council minutes) and local contact information (e.g., hotlines, historical landmarks, job lines, speakers). Several libraries can develop rich local resource databases collaboratively once the objectives and protocols are established. The product could be an Access file, updated and e-mailed monthly, or a FileMakerPro file linked to the Internet.

Libraries also collect stories and add them to their collections. Even in "older" days, students used tape recorders to capture oral history. Later they videotaped these interviews. Now those histories are appearing as video clips on library Web pages. School and higher education libraries can help train students in interviewing and taping techniques, then donate their efforts to the public library or local historical society (often connected to the public library).

Training is another service, both for staff and patrons. Web tutorials increasingly appear on public and staff Web sites. Videoconferencing services are also being offered by both schools and other libraries; this communication channel again provides personal and professional development for staff and public. For those who want and need that face-to-face technology training, collaboration facilitates the process through the use of teen tutors. These technologically literate youngsters can coach patrons of different ages, conduct formal workshops, and provide leadership for after-school homework centers. Teens can also develop Web pages for the library media center.

Advocacy

Libraries cannot afford to remain passive, even though well-meaning, institutions. Nor can they operate alone. When large campaigns are called for, the collective size of several library staffs makes substantial efforts feasible. Libraries must support each other when their existence and financial backing may be threatened. In addition, as major issues such as equity and intellectual freedom affect libraries of all types, all players should coordinate their efforts—and technology helps. Consistent messages can be crafted online and with groupware. Public service announcements can be developed cooperatively and disseminated through a variety of media: audiotape for radio, videotape, and telecommunications.

Although the preceding scenarios focus on internal matters, libraries can also play an important advocacy role in the larger community. The library remains a neutral site for open intellectual discourse. With the advent of videoconferencing, different libraries can host discussions of the same topic or varying approaches to an overriding theme, such as economic development, while maintaining real-time conversations between groups and taping those discussions for future broadcasting opportunities.

Case Studies

The Public Library Association (PLA) formed a partnership with the National Institute of Child Health and Human Development (NICHD) of the National Institutes of Health to disseminate information about how children learn to read and to expand preschool services in public libraries. They produced a report, *Teaching Children to Read: An Evidence-Based Assessment of the Scientific Research Literature on Reading and Its Implications for Reading Instruction* (1997) and a video directed to community leaders.

The Marin Reference Network, composed of professionals from multitype libraries in Marin County in California, facilitates service to a wide variety of users. An early technology-based project was a union list of special collections and indexes. School library media teachers also developed a database of periodicals, which was made accessible to other types of libraries. These collaborative efforts laid the foundation for fax interlibrary loan. With a simple phone call or e-mail, libraries quickly deliver documents by fax to each other without bureaucratic strings.

With the establishment of the Library of California, libraries of all types collaborated in a variety of projects. One of the first was an electronic database of environmental resources. Cambridge Scientific Abstracts formed the foundation for articles and research studies in that domain, and a well-assessed and indexed Web megasite offered useful links to environmental issues, especially on California topics. The Library of California also funded professional librarians' training for the effective use of these resources with their users. In the following year an economics-based database was piloted.

Illinois libraries have been working collaboratively since 1965 through regional library systems and the Illinois Libraries Information Network (ILLINET). Interlibrary loan has long been a mainstay of the partnerships, and it led to cooperative circulation procedures. Recently, a series of Find-It! Projects have used technology to facilitate the development of the Illinois Government Information (IGI) site, which is digitizing government documents, and an Every Library's Information (ELI) site, an in-depth directory of libraries. In support of these partnerships, the state library underwrites free access of OCLC First Search databases for all ILLINET libraries. Illinois is broadening its base by establishing no-charge group access capabilities to libraries in the Missouri Library Network Corporation (http://www.library.sos.state.il.us).

In Columbia, Missouri, a community network called the "Electronic Super Highway" provides public remote access to public information, a community services directory, curriculum materials, full-text periodical databases, and news stories. This project involved the Columbia Public School District, the city of Columbia, the local public library systems, and the University of Missouri. Teachers, in particular, are very interested in this service, and attend hands-on training sessions; school library media teachers provide them with ongoing support.

Libraries for the Future promotes public libraries through research, education, advocacy, and model projects. Its community relations arm, ACCESS, focuses on low-income neighbors to increase access to information and library services. It works with schools, business, and government groups and has created a leadership forum to analyze best practices. Los Angeles is one ACCESS site for school-library media center collaboration; through their partnership, teacher teams are creating templates to incorporate technology into the curriculum, and students are conducting online research and developing telecommunications skills (Libraries for the Future, 1998a, p. 28).

Close Up

The following report demonstrates technology-age resource sharing and acknowledges the strengths of different kinds of libraries. This project was made possible through a regional multitype library infrastructure. An earlier county-wide version of this service provided the model for the larger-scale work.

Connections: Opening Greater Bay Area Libraries to Students and Teachers (1998)*

Introduction

This Greater Bay Area Library Council (GBALC) project is designed to deliver article information to students and teachers in participating Greater Bay Area schools and community college libraries (K–14). Participation is voluntary. Librarians in participating institutions will receive faxed delivery of articles ("known item citations") in periodicals they don't own, but which are owned by one of the host libraries. To qualify for the project, a K–14 institution must have a librarian and pre-existing "high" tech capabilities: at a minimum, fax sending and receiving equipment in a location accessible to the librarian.

Purpose

The purpose of this pilot project is to determine the demand for information access and delivery in the Greater Bay Area for K–14 students and teachers, and to test the effectiveness of one information access and delivery model.

Scope

Participating host libraries will supply up to five article requests per week from any participating school/community college library. Host libraries will provide school/community college libraries electronic access to their holdings, when possible, for verification of potential requests. Printed periodical lists may be available from some host libraries. Transmission of article requests will be via

*Reprinted with permission.

fax, and articles will be faxed to the requesting library. Other electronic transmission methods are encouraged, but not required.

Project Organization and Oversight

The GBALC Document Delivery Working Group will provide oversight for all aspects of the project. Specific Working Group members will deal directly with designated librarians from school/community college libraries to refine operational processes and protocols as necessary.

Measurements

The following statistics will be collected:

Host Libraries:

information associated costs (telecommunication, photocopy, etc.)

number of schools/community colleges requesting articles

number of requests received/filled

reasons for non-fills

turnaround time as measured by date/time request is received electronically, actual time working on request (verification, pulling, duplication, sending), date/time material is transmitted electronically

School/Community College:

information associated costs (telecommunication, etc.)

number of requests submitted by host library

number of requests filled

turnaround time as measured by date/time request is sent electronically and date/time material is received electronically

TEAMING WITH COMMUNITY AGENCIES

11

The school functions as a community entity, so it needs to respond to those local needs as well as lead in local empowerment. The school should model effective community action. Schools know that collaboration can result in deep-discount group purchases, greater leverage in decision making, cost-effective resource sharing, and efficient training. Although the local community comprises several types of groups as well as individuals, an overall dynamic exists in a community, which should be assessed and optimized to develop good partnerships.

The Role of the Individual

Humans are social beings. They usually live in communities and are certainly affected by communities in particular and society in general, even if living in the wilderness. Each person belongs to some kind of group, usually several of them: from nuclear family to business, from a bowling league to an ethnic group. The more individuals connect meaningfully with community groups, the more they can influence their personal standard of living while helping shape local values and priorities. Each person has the ability to act as a partner or a facilitator of partnerships.

In the world of technology, individuals bring their own capabilities, resources, and interests to the community table. In turn, the community's technological status affects the individual's ability to make use of technology. If the local government blocks cable or telephone installation, many households may have limited access to the Internet. This limitation, in turn, can affect businesses that want to expand into e-commerce. The community at large then may spiral down in terms of economics as competing communities support such technology and achieve more financially. Thus, collaboration is a key to individual and community success.

113

What Are Communities Made Of?

In this chapter, "community" is defined as the local government jurisdiction, such as a town or city. Communities contain several kinds of groups that may or may not work together. Before the library media teacher—and the school at large—can partner with the community, they must identify and assess the local key constituents by consulting any of several sources, such as the following:

Census tracts, to obtain demographic statistics

Telephone directories, to locate government agencies and other services

Local newspapers and other mass media, to identify supportive businesses and key community issues

Chamber of commerce and tourist bureau documents, to identify leading individuals and groups

Public library archives, to examine public documents and local history

Real estate offices, to identify local highlights

Neighborhood group discussions, to identify local interests and concerns

Maps, to locate main arterials and landmarks

In examining these elements, library media teachers should ask questions such as:

- What is the population of this group?

- What resources (financial, material, facilities, human) does this group have?

- What are the group's main goals and interests? What are the primary threats to the group?

- What are the group's natural affinities or natural competitors?

- How does technology fit into the picture of the group?

- How are decisions made?

- Who is the linchpin of the group?

- What role does the group play within the community?

- How are students affected by the group?

- How can the school—and the library media center in particular—affect the group?

The results of this environmental scan can be organized into a database for future applications. In the initial stage, the information can be sorted by different fields to make useful comparisons. For example, a number of entities might be affected by students because they are natural "hang outs" for after-school activity.

These entities might form an effective coalition to support library media center activities in the late afternoon. Institutions of a similar nature, such as cultural groups, might be joined to develop library cultural programs. Technology-rich and technology-poor stakeholders could complement each other.

The Role of Government

Senator Patrick Moynihan maintains that "all politics is local." Certainly, the community's legal governance body functions as a link between local concerns and regional, state, and national legislatures. In the Information Age, governments regulate public utilities such as electricity and telecommunications. They also establish building codes and regulations that can facilitate or hinder information delivery systems. As a coalition-builder, government agencies can develop coordinated Web servers linking public agencies, including schools and libraries. These communication linkages improve government efforts as well by

- keeping the population current about the status of transportation and weather conditions,

- helping the community respond effectively during disasters and other emergencies,

- helping to coordinate events,

- offering government services online,

- facilitating lines of communication between voters and elected officials,

- providing information about community demographics and laws, and

- helping employment efforts.

However, governments sometimes lag behind the rest of the community in terms of technology incorporation. Some reasons for this are

- lack of technical expertise;

- lack of funds to buy and maintain equipment, facilities, and technical help;

- bureaucratic barriers; and

- lack of clear policies.

Other community agencies might be able to help matters. As public and private stakeholders work together, they can leverage their influence and resources to facilitate training and resource sharing. They can apply jointly for grants and government investments to improve community welfare. In that equation, library media teachers can use their community database and other resources to research and analyze potential partners, effective telecommunications policies and models, and training opportunities.

On a larger scale, government agencies can form regional coalitions to leverage telecommunications lines and personnel expertise. In the San Francisco Bay area, "smart communities" are developing policies for telecommunications deployment and economic development. They are fostering regional library systems that can share Internet costs and technical support. They are facilitating communication across businesses so cable, telephone, and satellite industries can develop technological convergence, which can translate into coordinated efforts to bring technology into every home, public institution, and economic enterprise. With regional collaboration, the following community scenarios will become commonplace:

- Increased telecommuting, lightening traffic and increasing business productivity

- Just-in-time information about events, public services, and community issues

- Convenient shopping and public services

- Remote training and broadened educational options

- Seamless connections among education, agencies, business, and government

The Role of Mass Media

Local media can exert a powerful influence on the community. Libraries may be the information center, but media constitute the communication center. In one way, the library media center can be considered as content-rich and the media as channel- or format-rich. The media really are constantly looking for content, so partnerships between these two entities seem natural.

The issue, then, is "What is newsworthy?" The media want information on timely and significant events and people affecting the community. Each medium has its own priorities: Cable and other television stations want movement, particularly that which can be captured in short segments; newspapers want action words and images; radio wants action sounds and voices; magazines want in-depth stories. When the library media center changes or has a novel program, the library media teacher should routinely write a clear, concise press release to the local media—and consider calling the press for live coverage. Library media teachers should also keep a camera handy to capture those "special moments," especially for the local newspaper if a reporter cannot come to the event. Library media teachers can also get coverage through letters to the editor in response to community issues that affect the media center.

On a systemic level, the library media center staff can help the school by developing and maintaining a database of local media outlets. This list can then be posted on the school server to maximize access. Library media teachers should also make the extra effort to visit these businesses to create a personal touch and to determine the best contact person. In that way, when a newsworthy item occurs, or the library media teacher wants to publicize a major campaign, information will go to the right individual at the right time so the news will appear.

Such interaction also helps when the library media center is attacked by some segment of the community. If the media center's relationship with the media is strong and stable, news sources will likely come to the media center's defense. They can quickly contact the library media teacher for relevant background details. It should be mentioned, however, that the primary responsibility for a positive "spin" still rests with the library media teacher; the reporter's ultimate goal is to get at the truth, even if it makes someone look bad. Following are some tips for handling awkward situations:

- Think before you talk. Be prepared for possible questions.

- Don't be manipulated. It is better to pause or to redirect a question than to give a quick, compromising answer. You can even say, "I'll get back to you on that point."

- Be careful of statements taken out of context. Try to stay positive rather than repeating a negative statement.

- Talk in sound bites: clear messages with intellectual substance and emotional impact.

- Be honest, sincere, and professional.

Remember, if you do not speak out in support of the library media center, no one else will.

Most professional library organizations have public relations functions and supporting documents. The American Library Association sponsors ongoing advocacy training. For the area of technology, the ALA publication *Libraries & the Internet Toolkit* (http://www.ala.org/alaorginternettoolkit.html) has tip sheets and sample messages.

Building a Sense of Community

Although a formal governing structure exists to "run" the community, those operations may seem ineffectual if the community itself is not responsive. With "bedroom communities," high transfer levels, and disenfranchised groups, there may be little sense of ownership in the community—and little sense of responsibility to one's neighbors. Problems grow and fewer groups work together to solve those problems or improve the local scene.

Even the best intentions and potential benefits will not bear fruit unless community action is well planned and executed. In 1998 the San Francisco Mayor's Office of Community Development realized that the change brought about by more local control of government funds required more coordination of existing programs and an increased neighborhood spirit. The office developed a set of principles by which to guide community projects, including

- support for coordinated community services,

- increased opportunities for economic and social inclusion,

- community-based goals and outcomes-focused project management,

- support for all types of families,

- emphasis on maximizing system impact,

- emphasis on preventative programs,

- sensitivity to and knowledge of cultural diversity and its positive impact on programs, and

- building on community strengths as well as responding to community needs.

Libraries are keystones in this process because they provide public access to a broad spectrum of users, reinforcing a community approach to information and democratic action. Many libraries already model collaborative models as they share services and expertise. Librarians know that no one institution can be self-sufficient; as different libraries identify their niches and their mutual needs, they can distribute efforts and finances efficiently to maximize their services. In addition, libraries enjoy a positive image in the community.

Likewise, schools provide one of the few safe harbors for some children. In most cases, schools are considered a "public good" even when they are not able to help every child fully. When schools and libraries incorporate technology, they can further expand their influence to help revitalize the community and help it coalesce. The following techniques exemplify how this works:

- Community events and services can be broadcast on the school and library media center Web server.

- Libraries can provide access to resources worldwide.

- Schools and libraries can provide community workshops on computer use.

- School-to-work opportunities can be expanded through technological tools such as videotaping and online conferences.

Measuring the Impact

To what extent do community partnerships make a difference? Following are some societal signs of healthy contributions:

Increased standard of living

Decreased digital divide

Improved education

Increased interdependence of community stakeholders

Greater and improved community services

Such community improvement requires ongoing assessment to modify or redirect projects to optimize the impact. Several factors merit close monitoring:

Outreach: Which groups are contacted? What communications means are used—and when? Which subgroups participate? What is the contribution and impact of each partner in these efforts?

Resources: How are resource needs identified and met? To what extent are resources supported? What are the nature, quality, and extent of resources? How effectively and efficiently are resources shared and distributed? To what extent do resources take advantage of the partnership?

Staffing: What expertise exists? What recruitment efforts are made? How is training done: in terms of targeted audience, trainer, resources, delivery system, evaluation? How is staff supervised, coordinated, compensated, and recognized? What is the contribution and impact of each partner in these efforts?

Processes: To what extent do processes address community needs? How efficient and cost-effective are processes? How do policies advance and support processes? To what extent does technology affect processes? How do partnerships affect processes?

Service: What services are the result of the partnership? How accessible are services? What are the range, depth, and quality of the services? How well do services address community needs? To what extent do services take advantage of the partnerships?

Case Studies

Remember Net Days in 1996 and 1997? Nationwide, tens of thousands of volunteers pulled cable and installed computer systems in schools to connect students to the Information Highway. The brainchild of Sun Microsystems' John Gage and KQED's Michael Kaufman, this community-based effort bypassed bureaucratic speedbumps to have a significant impact on education (http://www.svi.org/netday).

Bonita Unified School District created an effective technology program on a limited budget by using community resources. On a schoolwide basis, a focused effort was defined and parent volunteers were recruited. The school signed up for government donation programs (http://www.computers.fed.gov) and asked local businesses for equipment. The district then started a Hardware Club of parent and other community members to make sure donations would be "classroom ready." Parents were also trained to provide technical assistance in the classroom. By establishing a conducive climate and creating buy-in, the school was able to garner outside involvement and needed resources (http://www.bonita.k12.ca.us/ets).

The Whitefoord Community Program in Atlanta reflects significant partnership efforts. The K–5 school provides the following services, thanks to help from healthcare agencies, economic consortiums, the school district, Emory University, and other community organizations: summer reading program, after-school tutorials, child development program, dental and health clinics, job training, and family resource center (Furger, 2000)

Education Development Center, Inc. (EDC) became the lead partner in the America Connects Consortium by leveraging existing partnerships with the National Alliance of Business, the Alliance for Technology Access, HUD Neighborhood Networks, and the U.S. Department of Education's work with community technology centers (CTC) in low-income centers. EDC will provide expertise in educational technology, online training, and Web site management in libraries, schools, and other community settings (http://www.ed.gov/offices/OVAE/CTC).

Youth ACCESS is a national after-school program to help students acquire information literacy skills through publishing stories about positive role models. Developed by Libraries for the Future, this program involves local service agencies and community members. In addition, the sites are linked by the Internet so students can communicate with each other (http://www.lff.org).

Compton, California, in collaboration with the local transportation authority and the federal Department of Transportation, created the TeleVillage Project. It provides its residents with access to computers, training, and the Internet for a very low annual fee: $5 for students to $50 for businesses and organizations.

San Bernardino, California, educational institutions provide low-cost Web page development in exchange for business support. Together with government cooperation, they developed the Enterprise for Economic Excellence (EEE), which provides Internet service (with a percentage of revenues going back to education) and facilitates community efforts such as a state technology grant.

Seattle's Public Access Network (PAN) provides a Virtual City Hall where residents can communicate with city officials and get community information. By linking government agencies, PAN has facilitated cross-department content development and service transactions. PAN is accessed by businesses, individuals, the public library, and community centers (International Center for Communications). In turn, the Seattle Public Library's Web page provides access to information about foundations and grantsmanship.

The Chicago Community Trust includes a Blue Skies for Libraries program, which offers small grants to libraries involving the community in innovative projects such as a community garden, counseling, job readiness internships, and arts events (Libraries for the Future, 1998a, p. 18).

San Francisco, San Mateo, and Marin counties in California each held information technology summits that joined business and community leaders to share best practices in technology, discuss information technology opportunities and tools to improve the community's stakeholders, learn about funding resources, and develop public-private relationships. Businesses offered local teenagers technology training at school sites, and communities developed policies to facilitate telecommunications installation.

The New York Public Library's Schomburg Center for Research in Black Culture gives inner-city students access to its video labs. Panasonic donated the equipment, and Columbia University students give a hands-on video production clinic so students can produce a video newsletter on issues such as ecology, diversity, and literacy.

Echo Park's (Los Angeles) Central City Action Committee, the UCLA Department of Design and Media, Open Studio Los Angeles, and other community groups developed OnRamp@Sunset, which has taught more than 500 students how to express themselves through digital images (http://connectforkids.org).

Close Up

This federal grant proposal (co-developed by a public librarian and a school library media teacher) melds the work of community agencies, multitype libraries, schools, and a significant portion of the community: baby boomers.

Training Librarians to Work with Aging Baby Boomers

This project, entitled "Training Librarians to Work with Aging Baby Boomers," submitted under the Library Education and Human Resource Development Program (Higher Education Act, Title IIB Institutes and Fellowships), is to develop and implement a training program for librarians and other community agencies to work with aging populations. Activities of the project include training and services.

In specific, the training will focus on ways to work with community people who are known as "baby boomers." Training will examine the needs of this population and provide the basis for service for them as well as ways to incorporate their talents in library service and other community service to others. Sections will include 1) human development issues, 2) services to this age group, and 3) community volunteer opportunities for this age group. A train-the-trainer component will enable libraries to train and work with affinity agencies.

The library and community services component will arise from the training. Participants will target their services to meet the needs of this aging population through 1) collection development, 2) facilities accommodations, 3) referral series, 4) telecommunications access, and 5) programs. They will also create opportunities for this population to help the community through 1) intergenerational programs, 2) guest speaking, and 3) agency support (e.g., fund-raising, board membership).

Phase-in of the project will be as follows: 1) needs assessment of target population, 2) development of training modules, 3) train-the-trainer sessions, 4) training and work with affinity agencies, 5) development and implementation of services for the targeted population, 6) development and implementation of services using the targeted population as volunteers, and 7) development and distribution of a database of services and volunteer opportunities.

This project will benefit all libraries, community agencies, and library users. The affected target population, 1.8 million, represents urban, suburban, and rural communities of wide ethnic diversity. Represented in California is the Greater Bay Area Library Council (composed of five major multitype library systems and their associated member libraries) and associated library support groups, which have already begun a series of regional library projects; they also provide the basis for staff development and volunteer efforts. Community agencies, such as the Marin Center for Research on Aging and volunteer organizations, and local educational systems are collaborating with North Bay

Cooperative Library system (the fiscal agent) by taking part in the training and by providing services. This collaborative work takes advantage of the expertise of each group, as well as providing a solid clientele base for baby boomer volunteers.

Not only will the target population benefit directly, but also their own volunteer work in libraries will positively affect services for all ages. Baby boomers constitute more than 20 percent of the U.S. population. They are developing with aging parents as well as their own quality of life issues; boomers also constitute an underutilized group of potential volunteers and mentors in the community who can work with both young and old.

Funding ($82,000) is being requested for a project director, training developer, trainers, database developer, and supporting materials.

This project will pilot the train-the-trainer model for working with aging populations. As a result, other libraries and affinity agencies can use the model and specific training modules to provide services for this population and use them as community volunteers.

TEAMING WITH PROFESSIONAL ORGANIZATIONS

12

Professional associations can be strong partners for library media teachers because they provide leverage and support from a body of like-minded experts. When school library media teachers have no other paid staff in the media center, they can feel isolated. Professional library organizations offer a link to others in the field, be it locally or nationally. In addition, professional organizations in related areas, such as the Association for Supervision and Curriculum Development (ASCD) and the International Society for Technology in Education (ISTE), help library media teachers cross curricular lines and team up with other educators with similar priorities.

Most professional organizations offer the following benefits:

Professional periodicals and monographs

Web sites with useful links

Listservs or other group-based telecommunications channels

Continuing education opportunities such as workshops, meetings, and conferences

Grants, scholarships, and awards

Expertise and support on issues such as intellectual freedom

Policy statements and standards for issues such as outsourcing, staffing, and access

A lobbying presence for relevant legislation

Opportunities for leadership development

Most school library media teachers belong to at least one state organization, and many join the American Association of School Librarians (AASL) or other national organizations. One sign of professional conduct is supporting such organizations because of their high-profile role in the field. For example, *Information Power* (AASL & AECT, 1998) is a driving force behind many school library media preparation programs and state standards. The American Library Association (ALA)'s work on legislation and recruitment of diverse librarians points out the results of hard-working, committed volunteer members promoting librarianship.

Partnerships with professional organizations exist at several levels of commitment. At the most basic level, school library media teachers pay their dues to show support and receive association services. At the next level, they can participate actively by attending continuing education activities, joining listservs, and applying their knowledge to improve their school's library media program. They may also respond to membership questionnaires or participate in association research surveys. In both cases, the organization can use that information to target services or advance the field. Deeper partnerships develop as members join committees, run for office, apply for grants, and contribute to publications. By doing this they start to develop leadership skills, which can be transferred to school settings. Within the organization, they help shape state and national agendas. These library media teachers build closer ties with professional colleagues who can provide in-depth expertise and open network doors for them.

As members of a professional organization, school library media teachers can attain associative power to partner with other professional organizations to achieve high-level results. For example, ALA collaborated with the National Educational Association to get e-rate discounts for telecommunications. ISTE is a consortium of thirteen professional organizations, which crafted technology standards for students and teachers. Their joint leverage is compelling for educational efforts in this area. The site school library media teacher can take these standards to the governance board with the assurance that these competencies carry weight for board consideration.

Consider AASL's efforts to implement *Information Power*. This document, particularly its chapter on student information literacy standards and chapters on library media program principles, provides direction for school services. *At the national level*, AASL sought partnerships with likely organizations and encouraged its leadership to speak at these groups' conferences and write for their publications. AASL also solicited spokespeople from other organizations to support its positions. AASL produced publications that could be used with other organizations, vendors, and educators as well as by its own membership. Other national efforts aimed at school library media teachers included workshops, leadership training, identification of model libraries, and mentoring.

Widespread use of these guidelines did not end at the national level; *at the state level*, parallel efforts reinforced and personalized the message on a more immediate basis. Other state organizations came into play. In California, both the California Library Association (CLA) and the California School Library Association (CSLA) developed articles and conference sessions about information literacy and library media center programs. CSLA, in particular, has an active public relations committee that exhibits at professional organizational conferences and a strong curriculum committee that helped shape accreditation procedures. The state's department of education developed *Check It Out!*, a publication used to assess school library media programs, particularly as districts developed library media center plans to obtain state funding for resources. These organizational efforts help district and site library media center personnel create strong programs and provide models for neighboring districts to emulate. Through national links, school sites can participate in research that demonstrates the significance of implementing *Information Power*'s mandates. Partnerships at all levels reinforce each other and help all school library media centers foster learning communities.

Case Studies

Examples of powerful partnerships with professional organizations abound. The following case studies illustrate some of the benefits of such partnerships.

The California State Library, in collaboration with a joint task force of the CLA and the CSLA, developed a set of readings on joint use facilities and cooperative use agreements between public and school libraries. The state legislation passed a long-overdue bond measure (California Reading and Literacy Improvement and Public Library Construction and Renovation Bond Act of 2000) to fund library media center renovations and construction, with an emphasis on joint use projects. Its passage was largely due to the lobbying efforts of CLA and CSLA both as organizations and as a collection of their activist members. Joint use, although attractive to legislators, can be problematic for library media teachers because of governance and staffing issues. By using the expertise of organizational leaders, the state library was able to produce a document that helps developers become sensitive to these issues and prevent possible problems through proactive planning.

The Afterschool Alliance represents a coalition of public, private, and nonprofit groups that help communities develop after-school programs for youth. "Lights on After School" is an event template developed by the group, led by the National Community Education Association. The planning guide explains how to publicize and implement an awareness campaign about opportunities for student engagement after school. Another alliance project, Afterschool Ambassadors, identifies community leaders who provide programs for students. They are paid and trained by the National Center for Community Education to help others across the nation to duplicate their local efforts.

The Eisenhower National Clearinghouse for Mathematics and Science Education's mission is "to identify effective curriculum resources, create high-quality professional development materials, and disseminate useful information and products to improve K–12 mathematics and science teaching and learning" (http://www.enc.org). One of their major areas of support is professional development for teachers in the effective use of technology. They have created packages of print and electronic materials to train and inspire the school community. In addition, the clearinghouse offers substantial grants and grantsmanship assistance.

The National School Board Association has an Institute for the Transfer of Technology to Education (ITTE), funded by the National Science Foundation, which promotes "excellence and equity in education through the wise and innovative use of technology." ITTE's Web site includes many resources and links; in particular, the organization has developed a free online technology resource called the Educational Leadership Toolkit: "a collection of tips and points, articles, case studies and other resources for educational leaders addressing issues around technology and education" (http://www.nsba.org/sbot/toolkit). Users can participate in the association's e-mail group to converse with school board members nationwide, and members of ITTE's Technology Leadership Network can draw from the best practices database of successful models.

MOUSE (Making Opportunities for Upgrading Schools and Education) is a nonprofit organization that provides New York City public schools with technology resources and expertise through partnerships with industry. In one of its corporate partnership programs, MOUSE teamed with Arthur Anderson to create the Young Women's Technology Club. Technology CEOs install cable in schools, thanks to MOUSE. MOUSE's internship program has been featured in InformationWeek.com. MOUSE ensures regular communication through the newsletter *MOUSE Droppings* and conferences.

The American Association for Health Educators cooperates with public health departments to educate the school community. Noticing high rates of lead poisoning in Rhode Island, Joseph McNamera, health and wellness coordinator for the Pawtucket School District, obtained a grant from the Association for Supervision and Curriculum Development (ASCD) to develop a comprehensive school health education initiative. The sponsored activities included junior high student research on lead poisoning and presentations of their findings to elementary students, student displays at health fairs, and workshops for parents (http://www.ascd.org).

The Children's Partnership organization "undertakes research, analysis, and advocacy to place the needs of America's nearly 70 million children and youth, particularly the underserved, at the forefront of emerging policy debates." A major publication of the Partnership, *Online Content for Low-Income and Underserved Americans: The Digital Divide's New Front* (2000), surveyed the technological needs in communities and suggested opportunities for improvement. The Partnership recommended immediate local action and a national strategy using online tools. The book mentioned successful projects such as the Neighborhood Technology Resource Center at Chicago's Northwest Tower Apartments (http://www.northwest.com), which built an employment resource network of unique community assets; the LINC Project (http://www.lincproject.org), which provides technical help on-site and training to other organizations; and the Texas Community Networking Guide (http://lone-eagles.com/texas), which offers train-the-trainer modules.

The First Day Foundation (http://www.firstday.org) focuses on opening day events that involve parents and the greater community. The foundation offers do-it-yourself planning kits and links to other relevant organizations. Using the foundation's materials, schools have succeeded in getting parents to do research alongside their children and to donate money for parenting libraries.

The Alliance for Community Media (http://www.alliancecm.org) represents more than 1,000 educational, public, and government public access organizations and Internet centers to ensure access to electronic media. The organization promotes "public education, advancing a positive legislative and regulatory environment, building coalitions and supporting local organizing." One of the group's popular projects is the national Hometown Video Festival, which recognizes outstanding community production efforts. The Allen County Public Library received one of these awards for its *More Than Books* TV series that highlighted library media center events, people, and services.

What Makes Them Work

Partnerships with associations can constitute a powerful mechanism for school improvement. The classic study *Giving in America* (1975, p. 1) enumerates the characteristics of voluntary groups and associations that help such constituents be useful collaborators:

Initiatives: Because these groups need to listen to their own members and are not hampered by profit-line bureaucracy, they can experiment with new ideas and processes.

Public policy: As independent entities, groups can research local and national issues and make reasoned suggestions to governing bodies.

Alternative advocacy: Disenfranchised or marginalized groups can garner support from nonprofit organizations. What government or even schools may have overlooked can be brought into focus by library media center groups. For example, library media teachers as a group can push for equitable access and appropriate accommodations to technology for students with special needs. Small interest groups can bind together to create a more powerful voice.

Safety net for service: Especially in public schools, some services cannot be conducted freely because of government regulations. However, nonprofit organizations can step in. For example, the Catholic Library Association can deal comfortably with religious publications. Media literacy groups can speak to parents without infringing on freedom of speech.

Citizenship: Voluntary groups such as the American Association of University Women model good citizenship and can work with school libraries to offer volunteer opportunities for students; [the AAUW] group is particularly effective on voting issues and can sponsor student voting simulations and forums.

It should be noted that organizations retain their own identity and priorities as they work with others. The key is to find mutual goals and focus on them rather than to try to mesh every philosophical stance or insist on a lifelong partnership. A good way to proceed once the potential for collaboration seems feasible is to form a small group of key stakeholders who can identify needs, resources, and means of communication. They, in turn, can liaise with their constituents to educate them on the issues and bring more folks on board to address specific issues. Partners can help each other understand the issues and develop action plans. As a coordinated body, the coalition can produce and distribute products and conduct activities that further the joint agenda (Blake et al., 1985, p. 25).

Close Up

The following two resolutions show how organizations can publicly support libraries. The first example was written by a federal coalition of library support groups; the second was developed by a powerful national educational group. School library media teachers can use these statements to garner support from the school and local community.

U.S. National Commission on Libraries and Information Science Resolution in Recognition of the Important Role of Libraries in the Lives of America's Children

Whereas we have seen the recent outbreak of children venting rage and anger by killing parents, teachers and schoolmates,

Whereas we know that mental development, positive socialization and emotional stabilization must begin at birth if children are to grow up with full success,

Whereas we are aware of the uncertainties, hidden needs for information, and fears about being different or disliked in children, adolescents and young people; and

Whereas we are concerned about the needs of tens of thousands of young persons now in corrections or on probation who may return to destructive behaviors if they receive no redirection,

Be it resolved that the U.S. National Commission on Libraries and Information Science urges that our society—officials and educators at all levels, community leaders, parents and other adult caregivers, confidantes and role models—utilize the vast potential of libraries and support the current and potential abilities and efforts of librarians in assisting adults, youth and children to seek positive outcomes through wise use of information, and

Be it further resolved that, in seeking solutions through better parenting and learning experiences for young children and redirection for troubled older children and adolescents, libraries can be a major delivery point.

Resolved by the U.S. National Commission on Libraries and Information Science at its meetings on June 26, 1998, in Washington, DC (http://www.nclis.gov/info/childres.html).

National Education Association 1999–2000 and 2000–2001 Resolutions (http://www.nea.org/resolutions/00/00b-58.html)

Each year, delegates to the NEA Representative Assembly meet, discuss issues, and set Association policy for the coming year. Resolutions in 1999–2000 included:

B-57. School Libraries/Media Programs

The National Education Association believes every student must have a comprehensive library/media program within his or her educational setting. This program should include printed and nonprinted resource materials, instruction in library research and information skills, necessary technology, certificated librarians/media specialists, and educational support personnel.

B-58. School Libraries/Media Programs

The National Education Association believes every student must have a comprehensive library/media program within his or her educational setting. This program should include printed and nonprinted resource materials, instruction in library research and information skills, necessary technology, certificated librarians/media specialists, and educational support personnel. (80, 92)

B-61. Internet Access

The National Education Association believes that every school classroom, office, teacher workroom, and library/media center should have affordable, high-speed, seamless, and equal access to the Internet.

The Association also believes that education employees are essential to the development of an acceptable use policy (AUP) and to the appropriate use of the Internet.

The Association further believes that an AUP that requires the signatures of parents/guardians/caregivers and students must be in place before allowing student access.

The Association also believes that Internet access and activities should be age appropriate and monitored and should foster critical use. Any documentation material produced as a result of Internet access should be properly cited and comply with copyright laws.

TEAMING WITH BUSINESS

13

At a recent school board conference, a trustee asked me about the role of business in schools and school libraries. I said I saw many opportunities for engagement and mutual support, which pleased and surprised the trustee—who happened to be a businessman. "I like the way you think; it's not the usual response," he said. He asked for more information, and left me and my association booth satisfied—and eager to work more solidly as a school board trustee and community member.

Librarians sometimes view business collaboration with school libraries warily because they fear that "outsiders" will control the library. Because some nonpublic entities have actually taken over a school and managed it, library media teachers might well worry about their knowledge and support of the library sector. To mitigate such fears, library media teachers should work with the rest of the school to delineate the role and expectations of business partners before inviting them to the table. And library media teachers also must have a firm grasp of their own programs.

Businesses have a high stake in schools because they deal with the "products" of education. When a potential employee cannot complete an application competently or interview with aplomb, businesses turn that person away—a person who might have the technical skills that the employer needs. Most businesses realize that they do not have training in pedagogy and do not want to venture into that arena on the school grounds, but they do know their own business and can tell schools what skills and attitudes are needed to be prepared for the work world. Although schooling is not career-oriented, it does promote life-long learning and aims to help students make sense of the world around them. Because this attitude forms the basis of the school library media center instructional program, business and media center interests are well aligned. The challenge is how to optimize those mutual interests.

Mutual Benefits

Schools are community institutions. Despite population transience, most communities do have a base of stable residents and businesses. Employees' children go to the school; students become employees in the community. It makes sense for schools to be responsive to community needs and for local businesses to get involved in the preparation of their future staff.

What does business have to offer schools—and school library media centers in particular?

Money: Education can be a useful tax write-off. Positively speaking, local financial investment pays off in better-prepared potential employees. Companies with a reputation for helping local schools attract attention and may be viewed more positively by local government.

Material resources: Businesses often need to remain on the cutting edge, so they may donate quite adequate equipment to the school. In addition, companies may get samples, which they can relay to schools. Some companies may even practice corporate "tithing" to education, donating one copy of a software program for every ten purchased for themselves, for example. Businesses such as Pizza Hut may donate their own products as incentives for reading programs. Cable companies are required to provide one free drop line into every public school. Companies may also produce custom products for school use, such as teacher guides created by *Time* magazine and the National Hockey League! On a lower level of involvement, but still offering a useful service, companies may also host school Web pages.

Expertise: Businesses know their jobs, and they know the kind of preparation needed to perform well. As they work with schools, businesses can identify those courses that help students prepare for employment and can provide some assistance in those subject areas. For example, businesspersons can speak to classes, giving real-life examples of applications of curricular concepts. Employees can tutor students and train parents. They can advise co-curricular clubs, such as video clubs. On a one-to-one basis, businesses are increasingly mentoring students via telecommunications. With adults, businesses consult with schools on fund-raising or public relations campaigns.

Apprenticeships and internships: As school-to-career programs regain popularity, local businesses can give students experiential learning opportunities aligned with academic curricula. On a short-term basis, students can "shadow" employers, documenting their experiences to share in school settings. Teachers also can participate in summer intern programs with businesses, providing educational expertise to complement business savvy. One impressive school-based partnership was Kinko's for Kids. Students learned how to do production work, and the school was able to provide an on-site professional service at low cost for the entire school community.

Connections: Because companies belong to local business groups or professional organizations, they know others in the field who can lend support to schools. As members of a Friends group, businesspeople can help put the library media teacher in touch with, for example, a key person to obtain grants.

On their part, school libraries can be attractive partners for businesses. The following list includes selling points for library media teachers seeking support from the corporate world:

Information: The library media center collects and accesses a wide variety of resources that support the curriculum. The library media teacher also stays current about school priorities and activities—as well as maintaining archives of important school documents. Businesses may need to research the school's history for a community celebration or look up information about teen habits.

Expertise: The library media teacher understands and optimizes the research process and can instruct people about information literacy. The library media teacher knows how to incorporate technology into the curriculum and can coach businesses as well as faculty. The library media teacher also knows the entire student and staff population and can match information needs with user capabilities. The library media teacher can set up speakers' bureaus or co-sponsor parenting workshops.

Equipment: Hopefully, the library media center represents the technological vanguard at school. The media center should make available to the school community not only computer systems but also TVs and VCRs and digital, audio, and video equipment. Students can interview businesses and add the documentation to the media center collection. Performing artists can showcase their work in the media center, again with the added benefit of being videotaped for community-based cable stations.

Facilities: Library media centers may have meeting space to host community-based programs. Regardless of size, media centers provide a neutral and open space for community discussion.

Audience: Schools have "captive" audiences that provide businesses with one-stop communications access. In some schools, businesses use students for market surveys or as software program beta-testers; in return, the resulting products are donated to the schools. On a more proactive basis, students help businesses mount Web pages through their Web design classes.

Reputation: On the whole, school library media centers have a positive image. Library media teachers are helpful and knowledgeable people. They love books and learning. Media centers are intellectual havens and places where people want to congregate and feel safe. Businesses can leverage those facts when they partner with library media teachers; being a library media center supporter looks good to the public: Doing well by doing good.

What NOT to Do

Although partnerships with business can benefit both parties, the path to success can be fraught with pitfalls. Usually these disasters have to do with unrealistic expectations or unclear communication. Preventative measures will usually iron out the problems.

Businesses do not want to be treated as benign money bags that the library media teacher continuously asks for donations, no questions asked. This is not a partnership. Businesses need to see that their investment is sound and provides a good return for the outlay. For example, a business would be annoyed if its money was spent to buy *Thrasher* magazine (unless the company was in the skateboard business) or to purchase drinks for teachers on Fridays. A company would be pleased if money was spent on a local newspaper subscription (especially if a sign was posted listing the company's sponsorship) or on food for a breakfast meeting of local businesses and the library media center staff. Businesses welcome the opportunity to provide computer software, knowing that their employees' children will benefit from its use and that the software is a standard one in their office; in effect, it helps students prepare to work successfully in their offices.

For their part, libraries do not want strings attached to business donations. For example, many libraries did not participate in the Channel One television donation because they did not believe in showing advertisements as part of the educational day. Likewise, library media teachers are sometimes reluctant to take free book covers promoting a local business or to serve as solicitors for one brand of encyclopedia to get a free set. The latter issue, especially, impinges on library media teacher ethics, which state that professionals help users evaluate resources by offering criteria and that commercial promotion is unfair practice.

Businesses do not want a single-shot transaction—or repeated requests—without some sort of followup. Whenever a donation is received, the library media teacher should thank the business, publicize the donation, and tell the business the impact that the donation has had. When libraries ask the business repeatedly for funding or other support, they should be think about developing a partnership with the company that lets the business play a more active role in the media center; otherwise, the business may think that the media center is taking it for granted. Perhaps a student aide can videotape a typical day in the business, and the media center can make that tape available to the school's career center also for student occupational exploration. The business could join the media center advisory board and provide input about community connections. When stakes are raised on either side, partnerships should be deepened as well.

Library media teachers do not like being manipulated by businesspeople, either. Businesses should not assume that the media center will take any machine as a donation; library media teachers must set clear system standards and policies relative to equipment donations and reserve the right to dispose of unwanted donations. Library media teachers do not have the authority to place a market value on equipment, books, or other materials donated to the media center. (This practice may be requested come tax time.) *Pro bono* work should not be quantified in terms of salary by the library media teacher, just the time—and that labor must represent the individuals' level of expertise if they are acting on a professional basis rather than as involved parents (who might shelve books or clip newspaper articles).

Positive Approaches to Business Partnerships

According to the Center for the Analysis of Commercialism in Education (CACE), the number of press citations about commercializing activities in schools rose 395 percent between 1999 and 2000 (http://www.schoolcommercialism.org). Obviously, school-business partnerships work well in many cases. Following are some pointers for optimizing these partnerships:

- Emphasize the links between business and family life. Schools can help employees with life skills. As parent employees are encouraged by their companies to become more engaged in their children's education, they feel better about their work—and the school feels better about the company.

- Build from strength. Schools are education and child development experts. Businesses know their field of entrepreneurship and the economic world. Schools can train employees as parents, and business can help in school-to-work applications and sound business and networking practices. Businesses also may have money or other resources they can donate.

- Have clear expectations on both sides. Make sure there are no hidden agendas or tacit assumptions.

- Check policies for possible conflicts between education and business. If businesses ask for special favors, use existing policies to back the school's stance. Have lawyers review any legal agreements.

- Be sensitive to time and labor issues for all partners. Outreach should complement or advance existing goals, not detract from them. Schedule parent meetings with work schedules in mind; use telecommunications for conferencing; have work-site parent groups; let parent employees have access to school resources such as computers or remote access to online databases.

- Maintain a balance of control and compromise. Aim for win-win situations, so neither side will feel slighted or manipulated.

Case Studies

T.H.E. Journal routinely reports on educational partnerships with technology companies. The November 2000 issue alone mentioned the following:

- AOL@School and the *New York Times* Learning Network (http://www.nytimes.com/learning) provide free age-appropriate, high-quality educational content for K–12 settings. The *Times* material focuses on current events and includes teacher and parent resources. A free Web site on news and information for middle and high schoolers, http://cnnfyi.com, is a partnership among CNN and Riverdeep Interactive, Harcourt, and HighWired.com. Follett Software Company also provides Web links; http://www.pathwaysmodel.com concentrates on literacy skills.

- 4Anything Network established a fund-raising program called Net Dollars 4 Schools, which gives schools a 12 percent commission for items schools sell through their online shops.

- A consortium of businesses, organizations, and educational institutions developed a statewide Web project in Vermont. Linked with school reform, programs use telecommunications and multimedia in the humanities (http://www.webproject.org).

- Gateway partnered with the Family Education Network to provide a community-based education program. Teachers get help integrating technology into the classroom, and schools get Gateway credit when those products are sold.

- Intel sponsors 100 after-school Computer Clubhouses by providing space and mentors to help youngsters learn about and use technology (http://intel.com/education).

Public access television offers free courses for students and other community members who are at least 16 years old. At San Domenico (California) School, students participate in week-long experiential learning activities. The library media center sponsored a video production class, which took place at Marin 31 television studio, the community program arm of the local cable broadcasting station. Students learned how to produce and edit videotapes and created public interest programs that were then broadcast locally.

With funding from the Kellogg Foundation, the Flint Public Library paid low-income teenagers to research local agencies and develop Web pages about community services. The Web Links project expanded its partnership to include middle and high schools as well as other community groups. Students worked with staff and teachers to digitize images and collect other information to produce the Web-based "Flint Timeline" (http://www.flint.lib.mi.us/timeline) to capture the town's local history, complementing the library's print archives.

Several companies (e.g., Hewlett-Packard, Gateway, America Online, and Cisco Systems) donate hardware, Internet access, and buildings in poorer neighborhoods. IBM has gone into lower-income schools and taught computer skills to families, then donated machines for home use. Cisco Systems has several R.O.P. programs in schools to train students in computer maintenance; schools and students get free equipment through this partnership and Cisco gains trained employees. Intel focuses on teachers, providing week-long training on integrating technology into the curriculum for leader teachers and library media teachers who, in turn, train peers. These teacher trainers receive individual computer systems, and the coordinating institution (usually a university) receives an Intel computer lab.

In Massachusetts, the Assabet Valley School to Career Partnership developed a community-based Web site that includes telementoring as well as local information about services. Of particular interest is the business section, which lists various ways in which companies can partner with schools (http://www.assabetcareers.org/business.html).

The Golden Gate Computer Society (California) is one of many volunteer business groups that recondition computers and give them to schools that ensure student access to the systems. They also welcome tech-savvy teenagers to help them on Saturdays to overhaul the equipment.

Partnershipamerica.com provides one-stop shopping and advisement for technology procurement. Led by Ingram Micro, this consortium of e-providers supports government and education through price comparisons, a variety of educational technology solution services, and online community and information services.

Apple Corporation models corporate world partnerships with education. Each year Apple awards and supports schools that want to develop innovative projects incorporating technology. The projects include Library of Tomorrow projects, Apple Learning Series (such as the Notable Book Student Project), and the Partners in Education initiative (between K–12 and universities).

Smart Valley (California) comprises Silicon Valley technology industries that provide computer equipment to local schools. Interested teachers apply for grants and receive "pods" of computers for their classroom.

Close Up

This press release deals with a regional effort among a variety of professional organizations and regional businesses to promote libraries. Both short-term and long-term business partnerships were involved.

Kids Connect @ California Libraries
(California Library Association, 1998)*

I am pleased and excited to share news about a "California look" to National Library Week! In collaboration with several partners, California Library Association is helping to sponsor KIDS CONNECT @ CALIFORNIA LIBRARIES.

Those of us who have been working on this effort wanted to encourage California libraries to take advantage of the national ALA campaign at the local level. And we also wanted to encourage all types of libraries—public, school, academic and special—to be involved in the National Library Week effort.

So we've created a California framework for all libraries to use:

a broader theme: Kids Connect @ California Libraries

a California "launch event" on April 10 in Sacramento

a media campaign to stimulate awareness and encourage contact at the local level

a Web site with great things for children, parents, librarians and teachers.

*Reprinted with permission.

The Web site is really something special:

- Libraries can use it during National Library Week to connect kids with great resources (there's a button just for kids).

- Libraries can use it with parents who want information about kids and the Internet (there's a button just for parents).

- Librarians and teachers can use it before NLM to look at all of the ALA National Library week materials (program ideas, logos, suggested texts for letters to the editor/proclamations/etc.) and/or to download text and graphics into their own computers.

- Librarians, teachers and those who support them can use this Web site to show the important role we have to create and organize resources in the new world of information.

You can read more about KC@CL in the press release below. And more information will be posted in the weeks leading up to National Library Week. Let me say how proud I am about the role that California Library Association has played in making this real. It has been a real pleasure working with other organizations and groups (and we all see other opportunities for continued collaboration).

I also want to salute PacBell and Jackie Siminitus. Jackie brought the vision AND a PacBell pledge of funding for media efforts to us and got the collaboration underway. And even now she is continuing to seek additional funding for a statewide TV/radio effort.

OK, California libraries! Get ready to celebrate National Library Week (Kids Connect @ The Library) with something extra and special:

KIDS CONNECT @ CALIFORNIA LIBRARIES.

Gregg Atkins, President California Library Association

For Immediate Release
For Information, Contact:

MEDIA ADVISORY

CALIFORNIA LIBRARY ADVOCATES ANNOUNCE
STATEWIDE ACTIVITIES TO PROMOTE NATIONAL LIBRARY
WEEK APRIL 13–19

"Kids Connection @ California Libraries"

For the first time, California library leaders and advocates representing the state's largest library groups are teaming up to promote National Library Week, April 13–19. "Kids Connect @ California Libraries" is the statewide, umbrella theme under which the library leadership groups are encouraging local public and school libraries, as well as academic and special libraries, to collaborate.

Plans underway include an official proclamation presentation on the Capitol steps in Sacramento on Thursday, April 10. State Librarian Kevin Staff will invite Governor Wilson to personally present the proclamation.

In addition, the groups have created a "Kids Connect" Web site (http://www.calibraries.org/kidsconnect), underwritten by Citibank, to inform librarians, parents and kids about activities at all types of libraries—public, school, academic and special libraries during and beyond National Library Week. The Web site includes tips and tools for librarians; a series of linked resources and elements of interest to children; as well as materials on library advocacy and ideas for parents on getting their kids involved in library and literacy.

The American Library Association (ALA) applauds California's "Kids Connect" efforts, which build upon the ALA's national theme "Kids Connect @ the Library." The California campaign extends their message to promote kids connect at libraries of all types—their school library, local public library college or university library, or special library.

Groups collaborating on the "Kids Connect @ California Libraries" include the California Library Association, California School Library Association, California State Library, California Department of Education, FRIENDS of California Libraries, California Association of Trustees and Commissioners, and Pacific Bell. The Oakland Public Library also serves on the planning team.

Participating Groups:

California Association of Library Trustees and Commissioners (CALTAC): Together with the FRIENDS of California Libraries, CALTAC represents the public interest in the public domain. The organization offers annual workshops in Northern and Southern California, and produces a quarterly newsletter, CALTACTICS. It also offers a trustee toolkit for library leadership.

California Library Association (CLA): CLA provides leadership for the development, promotion and improvement of library services, librarianship and the library community. CLA members are active in public, academic, school and special libraries throughout the state. In 1995, CLA celebrated 100 years of serving California libraries and librarians. For information, contact CLA headquarters at 916-447-8541 or info@cla-net.org.

California School Library Association (CSLA): "Learning through books, media and technology." CSLA's membership is composed of school library and media staff and others committed to enriching student learning by building a better future for school libraries. CLSA provides support for its members through communication, professional development, legislative advocacy and networking. For information, contact 916-447-2684.

California State Library (CSL): The State Library is California's public research library that helps a diverse people, their governments and their libraries meet their knowledge and information needs. The California State Library is under the direction of the State Librarian, who is appointed by the governor.

FRIENDS of California Libraries (FCL): If you are interested in public and school libraries in California this is the cyber-place to visit. The FCL California Library Advocacy Center is a resource and forum for those who value and support their public and school libraries, and to provide a virtual meeting place of the on-line community of library advocates. Contact http://www.friendcalib.org

Pacific Bell: PacBell's Education First initiative is a $100 million program started three years ago to help provide California schools and libraries with a digital on-ramp to the Information Superhighway by 2000. The program offers every school and library in PacBell's territory free ISDN lines for one year, technology workshops, and curriculum support. For more on Education First, see http://www.kn.pacbell.com

LEVELS OF
LEARNING
COMMUNITY
PARTNERSHIPS

14

How do school community partnerships grow? One child at a time. That is, the ultimate goal of each relationship is focus on student improvement for all. This end may be considered the "head" of partnerships. The "heart" of community relationships is the story of each individual child, accountability with heart. Keeping these two perspectives in mind, partnerships can maintain themselves even through rough times. Even when large groups collaborate, the personal touch makes the overall impact more meaningful. There are singular people at each level of partnership.

Project-Based Partnerships

Beginning partnerships can lay the groundwork for long-term efforts through well-defined, specific projects. When trying to size up a partnership, doing a concrete project with clear outcomes and parameters can ease the worry about unknown factors. Projects like the following lend themselves well to management software with defined tasks, responsibilities, resources, and deadlines:

Lesson plans

Speaker programs

Software fairs

School clubs

Videotaping school projects and events

Local databases

Workshops for students, staff, or parents

Web tutorials or hot links

Professional development mentoring

Grant development

Project Close Up

This alternative evaluation method encourages peer collaboration. In this case, the library media teacher gained knowledge from an experienced English teacher, as well as an entrée into the department. For her part, the English teacher was eased into the technology world, which she had feared. The parties learned from each other, gained skills, and deepened their collegial partnership, which helped with future projects involving the English department.

Alternative Evaluation Mid-Year Progress Form

Teacher: Library Media Teacher
Collaborating Professional: English Department Chair

1) *Briefly describe the teaching skills that are the focus of your effort.*

a. Improve and expand communication about library program
b. Increase technology integration into the curriculum

2) *What have you accomplished to date?*

a. Visited the following dept. meetings: English, social studies, applied tech, foreign language, math, science, where I showed books of interest to them
Solicited book suggestions from faculty
Did displays to promote school's Reading Enrichment Program
Produced/distributed monthly booklist
Created citation guides for MLA, Turabian, APA
Held National Book Week contests (including creating literary crosswords)
Developed research lesson on Fahrenheit 451, and taught class with it
Selected articles on professional topics and had them posted in Service Center and given to teacher study groups (particularly reading)
Joined Reading Study Group, and did research on reading
Lectured to Dominican College teacher candidates about teacher-librarian collaboration, incorporating literature across the curriculum
b. Produced and distributed monthly document on technology
Created and distributed workshop on how to scan pictures
Helped faculty and students use e-mail, Internet, Hyperstudio, and CD-ROMs
Coordinated/presented faculty session on educational technology options
Gave presentation on TAs in Technology pilot program and recruited one student into program
With student, developed a Web page on library resources
Collected and indexed good Web sites for research
Updated Site Council Technology initiative
Helped teacher write grant to acquire computers

Began work on networking CD-ROMs

Began learning how to install CD-ROMs on workstations

Began efforts to learn how to use TI programmable calculator

Lectured to Dominican College teacher candidates on reading and technology, incorporating technology

3) Identify any procedural problems or support needs you might have.

I would like an HTML software program.

I have difficulty getting sufficient time during faculty meetings to talk about new books and technology.

I would like more encouragement from the Staff Development Coordinator to schedule technology workshops.

Staking Out the Library Media Center

The American Association of School Librarians asserts that the main mission of school library media programs is "to ensure that students and staff are effective users of ideas and information." (AASL & AECT, 1998, p. 6) The library media program can be more effective through thoughtful partnerships. Too often the media center sets itself up as the handmaiden to the rest of the school, continuously responding to others' needs. If the media center is to maintain a leading role in the school, it must portray a powerful image and solicit support in its efforts to provide the best program. Sample technology-related collaborations that speak to core library media center services include

- indexed Web pages;

- evaluation of electronic resources;

- full inclusion of resources and services for students with special needs;

- instruction and application of intellectual freedom tenets (filtering issues, etc.);

- knowledge of and adherence to technology-related copyright regulations;

- flexible scheduling to ensure equitable physical access to the library media center;

- coordination and support of library media center/school programs, such as videoconferencing;

- virtual Friends of the Library; and

- support for full media center staffing (professional and paraprofessional team) with technical assistance.

Library Media Center Close Up

In this school, parent support is significant. A formal grant procedure helps the funders to allocate funds according to their priorities. This group also includes students, teachers, and administrators.

Parent Support Fund Grant Application

Application Title: Library Catalog Access Upgrade

1. What does this grant address?

The grant addresses the increased need for student and staff access to the library's collection. Presently, the library has only two public access catalogs, and students stand in line to get to the system they need to find the books they want. The library wants to add two public terminals.

Additionally, the library's main circulation/catalog computer is VERY slow, which causes long check-out lines, and seriously delays generating reports or importing new book titles (sometimes the machine is tied up for two hours!) It should also be noted that the dot-matrix printer is a six-year old donated machine, which is slow and clunky.

The library's computer that links to the SASI program, which is used to update student book accounts and for inter-school e-mail, is an older 486 machine that also needs to be upgraded. The station is also used for retrospective cataloging, which is making progress thanks to our part-time clerk's inputting, and a faster machine would speed up work here as well so students would have access to ALL the books in the library.

2. Describe briefly the exact nature of this proposal.

a. The library requests two Ethernet cards and network cables so two additional stations can connect with the circulation/catalog program itself. The library will move the present administrative Pentium system to the public access area. The library will get another donated 486 system to make up the additional public access station.

b. The library requests wood that will be built into a counter with a modesty panel on which to place the two terminals. The woodshop students will make the counter.

c. The library requests a Pentium III PC computer system to serve as the main circulation computer workstation.

d. The library requests a faster, laser printer that generates more professional-looking reports and notices.

3. Which students are affected by this grant? Include expected numbers.

Because every student uses the library, both for classroom and individual use, this proposal affects the entire school population. With more terminals and a faster circulation system, all students will be served more efficiently and will have better access to the library's resources.

4. *Explain what other areas of funding you have explored.*

The library applied for state funding, unsuccessfully. Maintenance money is for repairs only. Site Council money for technology is for operating costs at present. The library can get a donated station for one more access point. That the library is able to redistribute computers to cut down on new purchases shows the library's resourcefulness. That the library can get the workshop to construct the additional terminals' counter also shows cooperation and student involvement—as well as a cost-efficient approach.

Mutually Supporting the Curriculum

At the curricular level, the library media center can act as an equal partner in developing and supporting learning. Traditionally, the media center warehoused resources to support the curriculum. Library instruction usually focused on locational skills, such as the use of catalogs and indexes. Now the library media teacher should collaborate with teachers from the beginning stages of curriculum development all the way through student assessment and program review. With the advent of technology, the library media teacher can lead efforts to infuse the curriculum with technology.

This approach makes good sense because resources and learning activities shape instruction of concepts. For example, the teacher who decides to offer an elective unit on science fiction writing will be frustrated if the media center has few materials to support that course. When library media center budgets are lean, careful planning requires assessing the collection in terms of future curricular needs. A teacher who decides to incorporate many multimedia projects must make sure that the media center has the required software and peripherals such as scanners and digital cameras.

In terms of library media center instruction, knowing how the teacher plans to approach student work affects delivery of information literacy content. For example, if the teacher focuses on inquiry-based learning, library-related activities should align with that teaching philosophy. If the teacher wants students to ferret out facts from Web sites, bookmarking viable resources makes sense; if, however, the teacher wants students to analyze information critically, supplying Web evaluation criteria makes more sense.

For library instruction and resources to be effective, the library media teacher should examine student work to see how much learning occurred as a result of media center programs. Were there enough resources? Were they useful (i.e., current, reading-level appropriate, and aligned with the course content)? Did students know how to locate and use the resources? Could students cite them accurately? The answers to each of these questions require a different action plan by the library media teacher in collaboration with the teacher.

When larger curriculum issues arise, such as the revamping of departmental priorities or even the adoption of new textbooks, the library media teacher should work alongside the faculty to ensure student success. Ordinary changes in courses affect the media center collection, which must follow the moving target of curriculum. Major shifts can require serious weeding and acquisitions. If the library media teacher knows that curricular changes are de rigueur at a school, he or she might focus on acquiring content-neutral productivity software instead of content-specific titles and rely more on the Internet than on print monographs that quickly become outdated.

Noting that curriculum forms the core academic activity, and that technology is being asked to play an increasingly larger role in this endeavor, collaborative efforts in the following areas can demonstrate how the library media center can lead from the middle in terms of student success:

Information literacy scope and sequence

Media literacy scope and sequence

Workshops for students, staff, and parents on Internet use

Videotaping services and archives of best practices and student demonstrations

Collection of student exemplars for meeting technology standards

Archived lessons that incorporate technology

Professional collection

Technology fairs on assistive technology

Special interest groups (SIGs) based on technology tool, instructional approach, or learning style

Curriculum Close Up

The applicant asked the library media teacher to help her write a grant to obtain added equipment to revise her graphics design and photography curriculum. The library media teacher had used the teacher's room to advise a video club and was able to leverage her writing skills to get another computer for the media center and to encourage more research in the media center.

Kodak Grant Proposal

What is the goal of the project?

To develop the structure and resources to support student business development. Specifically, students will create business plans that incorporate photographic graphic elements to coordinate a variety of business communication products.

How does this affect the efficiency or productivity of teaching and learning processes?

This project provides a meaningful context for student learning—and teacher instruction, and teachings school-to-work skills. Because students choose their own business, they control their learning and thus expand their learning.

Which measurement criteria have you currently implemented or will you implement to assess student achievement in this project, and how will you determine whether you reach your project objectives?

The district has developed student performance outcomes for technology and school-to-work competencies. These are measured through authentic assessments, such as: "The student will produce a solo project that exhibits mastery of authoring tools, graphics, telecommunications, plus items from at least two different categories." Additionally, the student will "prepare a senior portfolio, including an artifact from a project that demonstrates some learned and practiced skill, an article from a team project highlighting the contribution you made to the project, and a self-evaluation of your work-based or service learning experience."

In addition, the district Business Round Table will evaluate student work through a rigorous presentation of products produced for a designated business.

What distinguishes this project from other educational approaches? What makes it innovative? Unique?

This project is based on a school-to-work philosophy. Students are engaged on an individualized program, which creates a personally meaningful project that prepares each student for a successful business participation. The project is innovative and unique because it explores the discipline-specific aspects of photography and graphics, it melds photography artistry/techniques and computer multimedia, it is cross-curricular, it incorporates research into business and graphic design, it involves the local business community, and it prepares students for real-life entry-work skills. Students also engage in community service through their graphics designs for local businesses.

How many and what kinds of faculty and students would be involved in this project?

The core classes would be the photography and computer multimedia courses. However, several other courses would be affected. Directly involved are Applied Technology students in computers and business. Because students would have the option of contracting with subject-specific teachers to design photo/graphic presentations related to businesses in their fields, every teacher would be potentially involved. Because their students would either pilot-test or use the products developed, all students in the school would be involved. The library (with its entire student user population) would be involved in the production and use of these projects. Of special import is the Senior Project option, which enables students to pursue a school-to-work in-depth experience.

Describe how you would use specific Kodak products to reach your goal. Specify the products, their quantity, the service, and the dollars that you are requesting.

The following equipment would be used to capture images for business products:

9 Kodak 4100 Advantix cameras (4 per lab, and 1 for library check-out)

4 Kodak Cameo Motor EX (mainly for B/W photos that students would develop)

1 Kodak digital science DC20 camera for library check-out

2 Kodak digital science CD50 zoom camera for high-end photo capturing

2 Kodak digital science DC40 camera for class use

25 single-use cameras for cross-curricular student use

72 rolls of Advantix camera film (24 each of 100, 200, 400)

3 Kodak clip art CD-ROMs to incorporate into business publications

25 copies each of the following: Photoshop, Illustrator, Pagemaker CD-ROMs

2 color scanners to import photographs into computer systems

2 ink-jet printers to print out business publications

24 VHS 120-minute video cassette tapes for student recordings

48 rolls of B/W 200 film for Kodak Cameo Motor EX photos

6 boxes of photographic paper (250 sheets/box) to develop photos

$1200 to print sixteen 4-color poster prints (two per cooperative business group)

$200 for Zip drive to store computer-manipulated photo images

$500 for Zip drive cartridges for students

$3,000 for Macintosh computer systems (one in library)

The school would appreciate service contracts to maintain equipment and technical assistance to make maximum use of the equipment.

Project Timeline

Acquire computer and software	Sept. 15
Upgrade existing computer systems	Sept. 15
Install software	Sept. 15
Design business-based projects	Oct. 1
Contact local business Round Table	Oct. 15
Advertise courses	Nov. 1
Coordinate work with senior projects	Nov. 1
Contact relevant teachers	Nov. 1
Begin photography and multimedia courses	Feb. 1
Progress presentation at in-service	Mar. 15
Presentation of business projects	June 1
Presentation of senior projects	June 1
Final assessment and report	June 10

Project Outline

Each student will research business graphics and create a business or work with an existing business that wants to revamp its product image and graphic theme.

In trio cooperative groups, students will develop a coherent and consistent photo/graphic theme that they will carry out in producing the following communications products:

> Letterhead
>
> Business cards
>
> Business mailer
>
> Business prospectus
>
> Business product (render in CAD)
>
> Product package
>
> Advertisements in a variety of media and delivery systems
>
> Video presentation (for sales or financial backing)
>
> Web page

Students may elect to contract with a teacher or librarian to design a set of presentations that incorporate photography and multimedia. This process teaches students the process for software development and, as such, should incorporate the following design processes:

> Content research
>
> Learning objectives
>
> Interactive design
>
> Visual reinforcements
>
> Programming details
>
> Feedback and record maintenance

Dissemination of Information

The project will be disseminated using the following channels:

> School faculty in-service meetings
>
> District in-service meetings
>
> County in-service meetings
>
> Articles in education magazines
>
> Computer-Using Educators conference
>
> National Computing Education conference

Assessment Rubric

Planning:

> – Student completes planning sheets.
>
> – Student does research to present factual, interesting information.

Design:

- Design reflects consistency and creativity.

- Text is legible.

- Information is easy and consistent to navigate.

- Design reflects planning for intended audience and purpose.

- Visual contrast between text and images is present.

- Color and artwork are consistent and complementary to content.

- Original photography and other graphics are used creatively.

- Placement and transitions are consistent except for special effects.

- Opportunities for user interactivity are provided appropriately.

Content:

- Understanding of topic is evidenced by factual, interesting details.

- Correct punctuation, grammar, and spelling are used.

- Information is organized clearly and systematically.

- Content engages audience.

School Initiatives

Schoolwide projects exemplify broader-based efforts toward building a learning community. If well designed and executed, these cross-grade/cross-discipline efforts not only reinforce contextualized learning, they also foster more collegiality. When initiatives work well, the school community should seriously consider either building another initiative related to the first or developing another independent initiative that can deepen these schoolwide connections. For example, schools may start with an "Every teacher is a reading teacher" initiative, which could segue into writing across the curriculum or veer into visual literacy or concentrate on shared reading experiences through a variety of media.

Technology in itself increasingly forms the basis for school initiatives because it use crosses curricular lines. But it can undergird other initiatives as well through its use as a communication and productivity tool. For example, a "healthy start" initiative can use listservs to facilitate discussion and dissemination of information, the Internet to research other "healthy start" projects, and Web pages to post appropriate articles and local links for parents.

In any case, library media teachers should participate throughout the process, from preplanning through assessment stages. Following are some ways in which library media teachers can contribute to collaborative efforts in general:

- Investigate and share successful—and unsuccessful—school initiatives that have occurred elsewhere in the region or farther away. With others, identify both obstacles and elements that work to optimize the school's efforts.

- Partner with library media teachers at other sites having school initiatives, and facilitate networking between other constituents such as board members.

- Locate online tutorials, continuing education opportunities, and experts in the field to help educate the school community about the specific initiative and how to address it.

- Locate resources to support and sustain the initiative.

- Collaborate with teachers to design and implement meaningful learning activities aligned with the initiative.

- Assess the impact of the initiative and explore ways to improve efforts.

The type of initiative determines the nature of participating partnerships. In some cases, a core of individuals will manage the initiative; other personnel should just recognize their efforts rather than spend lots of time planning or implementing the project itself. Developing rubrics exemplifies this type of initiative. In other cases, broad-based ownership of the initiative is required, but each person is only required to contribute a little. Developing a culture of reading can be a relatively benign process. In still other cases, short-term but intense work by many groups is needed to get an initiative rolling; school bonds are typical of this kind of effort. In each case, the library media teacher should determine the answers to the following questions:

- How does this initiative affect the library media program potentially— both positively and negatively?

- What is my role in the initiative? What skills and knowledge as a person apart from the library realm do I bring to the table?

- With what group do I affiliate? What is my role within that group?

- What commitment is needed in terms of time, resources, and effort?

- How can this initiative improve other media center partnerships?

Initiative Close Up

To obtain additional state funds for media center resources, the library media teacher needed to develop a media center plan that demonstrated school community involvement. She used the school's initiatives as the starting point of the plan. In this way, she gained the buy-in of the school constituents and assured that the resources would be used effectively.

Library Improvement Plan

Needs Assessment

Redwood is a suburban, comprehensive public high school that began implementing site-based management in 1992. It enjoys a strong scholastic record and a supportive community. As the 1994 WASC self-study indicated, the 1,250-student body population is growing and becoming more diverse in terms of background and academic/social needs; about 85 percent are Caucasian (a significant portion of which are Middle Eastern), with Asians, Latinos, and Afro-Americans composing a growing percentage of students. In addition, the first class of ESL students was identified this fall. As the school has introduced more curricular options, the library has tried to address these needs.

Now, the 5,000-square-foot library media center includes 36,000 print resources and about 75 CD-ROM/software resources for most curricular areas, emphasizing college-preparatory materials. Instruction is content-embedded. The full-time library media teacher and support staff work with students, faculty, Site Council, parents, local librarians, and district personnel to implement individual, department, and WASC recommendations under the Site Improvement Plan, which includes the following initiatives:

1) *Reading:* provide structure and resources to facilitate reading comprehension and enjoyment

2) *Diversity:* recognize and appreciate student socioeconomic, gender and learning differences

3) *School-to-world:* teach STW/post-secondary transition skills

4) *Technology:* utilize networking services and incorporate technology across the curriculum

The library planning committee recognized several needs as the library tries to facilitate student success. These needs were determined through student and faculty surveys, use statistics, observations, faculty and governance meeting discussions, and formal evaluation. The following resource areas were found to be in critical need:

Need for more books in the areas of multiculturalism, school-to-work transition, and hi-lo reading to meet needs of culturally diverse, at-risk, and academically challenged students; also audiotaped materials to complement written books

Need for more access to electronic resources (and related equipment) to meet the demands of diverse learning styles

Need to expand the professional collection to facilitate effective instruction

Concurrent with these needs, library media center service should provide more instruction (and aids) for students and faculty in locating, evaluating, and manipulating information in a variety of formats. Such instruction demands more collaborative planning and teaching between the librarian and teachers to maximize effective library use and ensure information literacy.

Facilities renovation and redesign is also needed to provide a variety of settings for individual and group research and production: e.g., carrels, conference area, larger production area.

Library Media Center Vision/Five-Year Plan: "Connectivity—High Tech/High Touch"

The library media center's collection and services must be expanded to comply with site and WASC recommendations and be guided by ALA's *Information Power*. All students should be able to find materials that match their interests and capabilities, increase their information literacy, and produce meaningful projects. With more resources available to teachers, and their expanded partnerships with the library media teacher, the learning community will be effectively connected.

Over the next five years, the library will improve by achieving the following objectives:

> 1) *Increase reading comprehension and lifelong enjoyment* through expanded reader advisory service, reading areas, and focused reading experiences through coordination with teachers

> 2) *Enrich academic needs of culturally diverse and academically challenged students* through improved curriculum-based and personal-need collection development (e.g., post-secondary information, resources to match new courses, audiobooks, interactive software), collaborative instruction with teachers, and user-specific work areas

> 3) *Facilitate STW/post-secondary skills* through literacy instruction and articulation with local post-secondary institutions (such as College of Marin and Dominican College)

> 4) *Increase access to and incorporation of technology* through expanded networking and workstations, intranet service, and video-satellite communications.

Financially, the library media teacher and school will use local, state, and federal funds to carry out these improvements. The library media teacher will also seek grant sources and work with other school departments to procure and apply outside funding to improve the library media center. Meanwhile, the basis for improvement continues to be collaborative assessment and planning with the school community.

Use of the Grant to Obtain Goals

The grant will help achieve the above-stated vision because the money will be used to buy CD-ROM/software titles ($300), audiobooks ($900), and books ($3,800). These materials will be chosen to focus on multiculturalism/diversity, resources to match new courses, audiobooks, interactive software, vocational guidance/post-secondary information, professional reading, and personal interest reading. Selection will be based on reviews and student/faculty suggestions and will reflect teacher/library collaboration and compliance with state frameworks and standards. Most important, these purchases will be publicized and incorporated across the curriculum and in various school programs through teacher/librarian collaboration, student involvement, and parent participation.

Sample activities will include announcements/displays/publications, study groups and workshops, book discussions, and pilot lessons/projects.

The grant will complement and supplement other school support for the library media center. As examples, the library media teacher will work with

- the English department, to purchase multicultural reading materials;

- school and district technology committees to facilitate network access to technological resources;

- Staff Development and teacher study groups to purchase professional resources and facilitate teacher training/planning;

- the Long-Range Facilities Planning Committee to redesign and renovate the existing facility;

- local librarian organizations, to expand links between institutions; and

- local post-secondary institutions to articulate information literacy efforts and teaching training.

This grant may not seem significant in light of a 1,250-student high school library budget. But when one considers the positive impact on the school community of this recognition, the benefit is multiplied in terms of morale, pride, and sense of purpose. These additions to the resources are vital.

Evaluation

To evaluate the grant's impact on achieving the library media center's goals, the following measurement tools will be used to establish baseline and summative data:

> Circulation and in-house use statistics to measure use of purchased resources
>
> Calendar of faculty training and planning sessions, and class use of the library media center to measure increased collaboration and use by several departments
>
> Student and faculty surveys on library media center use to measure attitudinal change
>
> Teacher review of sample student projects using the material

In addition, ongoing observation by the library media teacher and other library improvement planners will apply to the process to meet student needs.

Whole School Reform

The seminal study *A Nation at Risk* (U.S. National Commission on Excellence in Education, 1983) signaled the need for schools to examine and overhaul themselves. Since then, schools have come increasingly under public scrutiny. Schools are being asked to do more and to be more accountable than ever before.

When considered within the context of the changing society, this responsibility can be overwhelming. Standards, on every level from district to national or international, help define those expectations. When those standards conflict with each other or fractionalize resources, the school community can find itself in a precarious situation. In some cases, schools address these issues piecemeal or go into crisis mode to stamp out educational brush fires. Other schools leverage these times of disequilibrium to take a systematic look at education and their community's needs: "whole school reform." Implicit in this approach is the importance of partnerships: All constituents must be assessed and brought into the discussion to solve educational problems.

Several recent educational reform efforts have attained national stature, based on their successful adaptation and adoption in several regions and educational settings. Most strong models have been developed by nonprofit organizations such as Foxfire, Sizer's Coalitions of Essential Schools, Levin's and Stanford's Accelerated School movement, Comer's and Yale's School Development program, Adler's Paideia, Boyer's and Carnegie's Basic Schools network, and Slavin's Success for All and its extension, Roots and Wings. When examining these and other plans, The NorthWest Regional Educational Laboratory identified several components that facilitated reform effectiveness:

> Measurable and attainable goals for student achievement
>
> Research-based innovative strategies
>
> High-quality, ongoing staff development
>
> Community, parent, and schoolwide support and involvement
>
> High-quality technical help
>
> Coordinated resources and assessment (http://www.nwrac.org/whole-school)

Technology both provides an impetus for school reform, because these new tools require a reexamination of teaching and learning practices, and acts as a catalyst for change because the tools facilitate communication and coordination. Technology allows one to dream about education's possibilities. Technology also offers a convenient "excuse" to address contemporary educational trends such as the following:

> Constructivist learning through multiple resources and various tools to organize information
>
> Individualizing instruction to meet learning differences through integrated learning systems, electronic diagnostic tools, and multiple formats to engage students
>
> Multiple organizational and progression structures through graphic organizers, presentation/authoring tools, and hypermedia
>
> Problem-solving approaches to learning through simulations, WebQuests, and computer-aided design

Collaborative work through projects that can be divided into discrete tasks and technology productivity tools that can merge or be worked on simultaneously by a group

Sharing of information through telecommunications, multimedia, video, and so forth

Authentic assessment through review by a larger audience, electronic portfolios, and expert systems

Library media teachers can certainly contribute significantly to school reform efforts through their expertise in resources, research sources, coordination, and technology. They can also spearhead community involvement through identifying and organizing potential partners. If a number of schools embark on systematic reform through such vehicles as the Annenberg Institute of School Reform, library media teachers can form a special interest group to share experiences across sites. BANDL (Bay Area National Digital Libraries) is such a group. The group has discussed ways to foster inquiry-based learning and information literacy, created Web pages, and given presentations at regional reform meetings in an effort to facilitate effective change.

Reform Close Up

Technology often acts as a catalyst for school reform. This plan reflects a school's reorientation of education to align with outcomes-based learning. It also shows the school's new acceptance of school-to-world transition needs. Furthermore, the plan uses technology to cut across disciplinary lines that had blocked progress.

High School Technology Plan

The new Technology Plan bases its mission on the district's culminating student outcomes:

- Use technology to access information, analyze and solve problems, and communicate ideas.

- Demonstrate school-to-work/post-secondary transition skills and knowledge.

The plan will also be coordinated with the district technology vision statement.

Goals and Objectives

1.a **Technological resources will be**

- used to enhance and enrich learning opportunities for students in all areas of the curriculum,

- used to increase the effectiveness and productivity of staff, and

- used to prepare students for continuing education and for the world of work in the twenty-first century.

1.b **Staff development will**

- support and encourage effective, creative uses of technology;

- provide staff with a variety of ways to learn how to use technological resources as part of the regular performance of their assigned duties and responsibilities;

- provide in-service support by site or department, based upon needs; and

- implement a "trainer of trainers" model within each department and at the site.

Educational Strategies

2.a Technology in classroom/lab instruction will facilitate structured educational experiences

- to access site-based and remote resources,

- to facilitate problem solving,

- to communicate effectively and creatively, and

- to develop lifelong career knowledge.

2.b Technology will be coordinated site-wide to facilitate

- staff training and coaching,

- expand TA training and utilization,

- an electronic bulletin board/in-house e-mail for students and staff,

- CD-ROM downloading for lab use,

- acquisition and inventory of nonprint resources, and

- a regular maintenance and upgrade schedule for hardware and software.

2.c Technology will improve staff productivity by

- facilitating teacher attendance reporting, grades, communication, and instruction; and

- increasing staff access to telecommunications for research and communicating.

Action Plan

The following issues will be addressed in enabling the technology goals to be accomplished. Work will be done in cooperation and coordination with the site Technology Committee, Site Council Department Chair Council, departments, administration, staff development coordinator, and the instructional computer specialist.

3.a **Staff development:**

- Make greater use of county site-based technology cadre members.

- Train all new teachers about educational technology, especially lab use.

- Develop means to help all teachers progress in meeting NCATE standards about technology use (e.g., train-the-trainer model, variety of formats for learning).

- Develop and maintain resource list of in-house technology experts.

3.b **Curriculum:**

- Implement the district culminating student outcomes plan.

- Assess and modify current offerings (e.g., computer literacy, computer applications).

- Explore/implement new courses such as multimedia and music composition.

- Expand the student computer Tech Assistant (TA) program.

- Expand the 2 + 2 program in computer technology.

- Increase internships.

- Link courses to take advantage of technology (e.g., teach tech skills in computer applications class and use the skill in a communications class).

- Coordinate assignments/projects to maximize student effort (e.g., combine math and science skills using CBL probes; apply authoring skills to social studies presentations).

3.c **Material resources:**

- Investigate multiple-copier purchases for site.

- Develop regular maintenance and upgrade schedule for hardware and software.

- Investigate purchasing data projectors.

- Explore the feasibility of establishing a state-of-the-art language lab.

- Explore the feasibility of getting more network lines or modems into more classrooms.

3.d **Services:**

- Develop student portfolios using high-density storage devices.

- Inventory nonprint resources, particularly software (and licenses).

- Establish listserv/in-house e-mail for students and staff.

- Provide for CD-ROM downloading for lab use.

- Explore the feasibility of computerized attendance and grading for all teachers.

- Explore the feasibility of remote access to school computers.

3.e. **Funding:**

- Maintain a $20,000 budget for maintenance and repairs (may have to be increased).

- Develop a yearly budget to cover upgrades and replacements of software and hardware.

- Explore grant and other outside funding opportunities.

- Explore business and other community partnerships, such as Autodesk.

Phase-in of the Plan:

4.1 **Ongoing**:

- Train staff in technology skills and incorporation into the curriculum.

- Review and revise technology-related courses.

- Explore possible funding sources.

- Explore community partnerships.

4.2 **Phase #1**:

This phase establishes the structure and baseline for future work.

- Set up technology staff development schedule and resource list of experts.

- Train all new teachers in technology, especially lab use.

- Train teachers about district technology outcomes.

- Expand student technology options: TAs, community interns, 2+2 programs.

- Inventory software (including licenses) and other nonprint resources; produce a database.

- Develop a plan for upgrading and redistribution of current computer hardware.

- Investigate purchasing data projectors.

4.3 Phase #2:

This phase begins the expansion and outreach to achieve the next level of technology implementation.

- Develop a staff development plan to enable teachers to meet NCATE standards.

- Develop links between courses to maximize technology applications by students.

- Develop in-house e-mail and a listserv.

- Develop student portfolios using high-density storage devices.

- Develop remote access to selected school resources, such as CD-ROMs.

- Explore the feasibility of computerized attendance and grading for all teachers.

- Explore the feasibility of establishing a state-of-the-art language lab.

- Explore the feasibility of getting more network lines into all classrooms.

Shaping the District

Districtwide collaboration makes sense. Usually the school district is the official governing agency, with its board of trustees. Be it a small high school district or a huge K–12 district, coordinated efforts help address equity issues and provide a broader base of support and resources. During bond campaigns and redistricting, community interest runs high, but in stable times district issues can "fall off the radar screen" for the community. Awakening the general public only during crises is not a smart political move, nor does it recognize ongoing district support and student achievement. The best time to nurture partnerships is during good times, particularly when districts want to ratchet up success. Building on a solid foundation, districts can use their infrastructure to develop creative solutions to potential issues.

In districts, several elements shape library media center programs: the existence and role of a district library media teacher, the existence and roles of site library media teachers/media center staff, acquisition and processing procedures (centralized or site-based); possible coordination of program and staff development policies; and planning. In these days of site-based management, local control and direction typically override district library services. However, some thought should still be given to the cost-effectiveness of centralized reviewing and cataloging. Library media teachers across the district should meet regularly to keep each other abreast of issues and to develop districtwide projects, particularly ones that take advantage of technology, such as the following:

Union catalog of periodicals

Deep discounts for district-wide subscriptions, particularly for online databases

Database of local resources

District library Web pages

Databases of reviews

Coordinated public relations

Online staff development

Technology grantwriting

Fax-based (or computer-scanned) interlibrary loan

Centralized duplication services (e.g., CD-R, videotape)

Of course, a more systemic collaborative approach uses a districtwide library plan. In California, substantial state funds for library resources are tied to district library plans. This forward-thinking approach has brought community members to the library table for the first time in some cases. In support of this effort, library media teachers in Marin County, as well as other counties, provided workshops for site and district leaders on how to develop media center plans involving all constituents. In some cases, administrators awoke to the need for professional library media teachers and started exploring ways to fund that now-necessary position.

District Close Up

The library media teacher in this example coordinated a day-long series of technology workshops that used subject faculty with technological expertise. Her prior networking experiences facilitated her contact and work with these model teachers and helped the entire district faculty see how technology could be integrated into the curriculum. The library media teacher also conducted one of the workshops.

District Teacher Technology Workshops

Developing Multimedia Projects

In this workshop participants will learn to use a "10-step Development Process" as a guide to staff/student multimedia projects. They will see a CD-ROM that consists of a number of projects developed using this guide. Using the guide, HyperStudio, and Kid Pix, attendees will break into small groups to start developing a small presentation.

Desktop Publishing with PageMaker

Want to create a professional-looking newsletter? Want your students to develop a classy publication? PageMaker is a sophisticated desktop publishing program that can be incorporated into the curriculum. Attendees will have hands-on experience exploring Pagemaker's textual and graphic features.

Entering the Internet

Ready to enter the Information Highway? This session will help participants get into gear to enter the fast lane of international communication. Explore first-hand the mysteries of e-mail, navigation strategies, bookmark milestones, URL destinations, and downloading. Yahoo!

Behind the Door: Using Windows

What makes those IBM-compatible machines work? Attendees will learn how to install and access computer applications, maximize system performance, and generally "read" and manage hard drives using Microsoft's Windows. Get those fingers ready to practice typing and pointing!

Getting Data into Shape using Spreadsheets

Want your students to compare statistics and make predictions using numbers? Computerized spreadsheets are an effective means to organize and describe numeric data. Participants will use ClarisWorks to practice creating spreadsheets, using arithmetic functions, and transforming data into graphs.

HyperLearning through HyperStudio

HyperStudio is a simple authoring program that allows the user to link text and graphics in an open-ended manner. Participants will create simple stacks and will learn how to incorporate them into fun projects for students to develop.

Probing Science

Educational technology offers interactive ways for students to explore scientific concepts. Students will work with computer-connected science probes, application programs, and laserdisc resources. Be prepared to come away with lots of ideas!

Getting Graphic with Calculators

Graphing calculators are becoming a standard learning tool in mathematics and science. Participants will learn how to operate these sophisticated calculators and how to incorporate them into a variety of mathematical settings.

Getting to First Base with Databases

Test hypotheses with databases. Participants will use Works to have hands-on experience delineating data into fields, creating databases, sorting factors, retrieving information, and making inferences from their findings.

Making your Point with PowerPoint

Design dynamite presentations with the help of PowerPoint. Part of Microsoft's Office suite of applications, PowerPoint is an easy way to create "slides" for instruction. Participants get to try their hand using built-in templates to produce professional-looking shows.

Improving the Community

Although schools exist within the community, they sometimes seem to operate alongside rather than in collaboration with it. Because schools prepare students to work within some community, even if it is not that specific one, they would do well to improve the climate in which those students live the rest of the time. For example, real estate agents know that good schools attract educated, more well-to-do families. Although the main "business" of schools is the preparation of its students, still, schools can proactively affect the community and help shape its direction.

Traditionally, schools have helped the community through adult education opportunities and recreational access. Millions of immigrants have learned English through public school outreach. The school baseball field has long been a summer community center for neighborhood games. Nowadays, schools offer after school programs as a positive alternative to gang activity and as a support to two-income families. Additionally, schools increasingly offer evening library media center hours and even midnight basketball as healthy community services. Another way in which modern schools have approached community involvement is through coordinated delivery of social services such as health and recreation. New school buildings are often constructed as part of a community center of recreation and public service. Day care centers provide training for high schoolers—and sometimes service to teenage parents. Medical services help get youngsters started on healthy habits and provide preventative education and interventions as needed, such as smoking cessation programs. Schools collaborate with businesses and agencies to offer training in parenting, technology, and other life skills.

School library media teachers have a distinct advantage in these partnerships because they share professional functions and values with librarians in other settings. This natural affiliation facilitates networking across institutions. For example, if all library media teachers were to develop databases of experts associated with their programs, then meld those databases into a community-wide resource, they could develop a ready-to-go, broad-based source for many community projects. Even sticking to "library business," local library networks can improve the community in a number of ways:

> Joint cultural events
>
> Community-based teen volunteer program
>
> Coordinated year-round reading programs
>
> Community-based technology training
>
> Coordinated resource selection
>
> Community library media center Web page, created with links to specialized collections and services unique to each library media center
>
> 24/7 community reference hotline

Outreach projects beyond the normal media center role can further enhance the library media teacher's image and influence in the community:

- Contribute to a community Web page.

- Help develop a community-based telecommunications plan.

- Help community literacy campaigns.

- Help coordinate community volunteer services.

- Help with a community career fair.

- Assist in advocacy training.

- Contribute to voter awareness projects.

- Enable the media center to serve as a town hall videoconferencing site.

- Help coordinate interagency projects such as child wellness services.

Community Close Up

The following recommendations reflect the importance accorded school library media centers within the larger community. The author was a key witness in the testimony process.

1998–1999 Marin County Grand Jury
Marin County Public School Libraries
May 1999
http://grandjury.marin.org/1998gj/library.html

Recommendations

The Grand Jury recommends that:

1. Every school have the services of a full-time, credentialed librarian or media specialist.

2. The Marin County Office of Education implement an in-service workshop for librarians, principals and teachers to focus specifically on such issues as:

    Services of professional, credentialed librarians

    Spending levels for books and other library resources

    Library staffing levels

    School library hours

    Assistance and maintenance support for technical equipment

    Technical training of library personnel, including computer use skills

    Access to the World Wide Web and other information sources.

3. The Marin County Office of Education's (MCOE) "Public School Services, Programs and School Information" booklet provide the following additional information for each school:

    Whether the school has a library;

    When the library is open;

    Whether the school is staffed with a credentialed librarian;

    The hours each week the librarian works at that school.

4. The Association of Marin County Schools Joint Legislative Advisory Committee, the lobbying arm of Marin County schools made up of 46 superintendents and board members, work towards assuring continued yearly funding under the Public Schools Library Act.

5. The Marin County Office of Education consider creating the position of *County Schools Librarian*. This position should in no way hinder individual districts and schools from hiring credentialed librarians nor interfere with schools' autonomy in making decisions concerning their libraries.

Information Literacy Across the Levels

School library media teachers consider information literacy as a core component of library media programs. Although school communities increasingly value information literacy, they do not necessarily see library media teachers as its locus of control. Most classroom teachers still think of themselves as the prime instructors and consider information literacy to be part of their domain.

The library media teacher who touts information literacy as a particularly library media center enterprise will get less than optimal support. The library media teacher should encourage teachers to view information literacy as a wonderful vehicle for effective partnerships. At each level of involvement, information literacy lends itself to thoughtful planning and implementation, and in today's digital world, the repertoire of tools expands the possibilities:

Individual projects: Help a debate club learn how to research government documents online. Co-sponsor an author videoconference. Help a class learn how to import images into multimedia presentations. Advise a ThinkQuest team. Help create a Wellness newsletter.

Library media center programs: Link a computer lab and the media center for after-school research. Coordinate student tech teams. Collect student-created thematic "Webliographies." Team teach about technology-related copyright issues. Install reference and subject-specific CD-ROMs on the library network server for access on-site and from home.

Curriculum impact: Let students take online courses in the library media center. Coordinate an in-house broadcasting service. Train teachers in cooperative learning using technology. Help develop a technology-infused curriculum. Create a relational database cross-referencing information literacy with domain-specific constructs such as the scientific method or content analysis.

School initiatives: Network technology instruction. Create an interactive online book club. Spearhead a technology committee and coordinate technology grants. Collect exemplars of student work using technology. Provide technology to help students create electronic portfolios.

Whole school reform: Help research and analyze school reform models. Facilitate online community "chats" about school reform. Address digital divide issues within the context of reform efforts. Coordinate virtual volunteers. Set up a school reform listserv.

District efforts: Help develop a district technology plan. Set up standards for hardware platforms and software upgrades. Coordinate a summer technology academy for staff. Develop a Web hot list of district policies. Coordinate a software review service.

Community improvement: Help plan and produce cultural broadcasts on local cable stations. Help coordinate and archive student-videotaped interviews with local businesses. Train technology businesses in ways to optimize student internships. Participate in community technology policy development. Connect businesses and parents through technology classes.

Information Literacy Close Up

These consultant planning notes reflect a small rural school's interest in and support for information literacy and the library media center. The beginning impetus was a facilities renovation, but a more substantial project ensued as the consulting library media teacher worked with the entire school community to realize the need for information literacy skills and the resources to support them.

Library Improvement Plan: Consultant Notes

Process for Selection of Books

1. First priority (and biggest expense) is reference: Library clerk and neighboring librarian will weed on March 12. Needs include new encyclopedias, atlases, and dictionaries.

2. Second priority is nonfiction.

3. Magazine collection also needs to be enhanced: consider purchasing multiyear subscriptions for essential magazines, buying SIRS, asking students, purchasing new magazines with one-year subscriptions and evaluate them based on whether circulated/not stolen; have each school class contribute a subscription.

4. Look at biggest gaps in current collection: Library clerk and neighboring librarian will do on March 12.

5. Look at curriculum: Librarian consultant will lead discussion at faculty meeting March 28, 1 P.M., followed by SIRS demo (Library clerk will arrange.); will include discussion of how to talk to students about what they want at the library.

6. Get students involved: classroom discussion week of April 7, followed by student forum week of April 14 with selected students.

7. Librarian consultant will develop priority lists; library clerk will do ordering.

Redesign Physical Space

Meet with parent committee: principal will arrange within next two weeks; PTA president will join meeting if possible

1. Mirror reference loft with fiction/leisure reading loft.

2. Create comfortable reading area with chairs (no sofas, no wheels).

3. Get new magazine rack.

4. Replace stairs with ramps to lofts.

5. Increase shelving.

6. Between shelves place carrels for privacy and shelving flow.

7. Incorporate oversized books into regular shelves; possibly create small shelf on top.

8. Install computers for students to use, especially because technology room is sometimes locked; also possibility of a VCR area.

9. Have several large tables available for classes to come in and work in library; consider placing these away from student lounge area to discourage socializing and encourage study.

Next Steps

- Hire district librarian (.8 position) principal with board; principal will contact librarian consultant with information so we can get the word out for applications.

- Work with district librarian and library clerk to develop a plan for sustaining excellent services and an up-to-date collection at school.

- At completion of project, have a literary walkabout with all faculty; split into 2–3 groups (led by librarian consultant, library clerk, possibly district librarian) to introduce and familiarize them with new collection, possible ways to use it.

- Grand opening party—invite parents, students, thank parent and community volunteers.

Technology Standards Across the Levels

Most jobs need some kind of technical expertise, even if it is only use of machinery or simple word processing. Technology is a way of life for most of the United States, if in no other form than the telephone and the television. Wise use of technology can help democracy; its abuse can threaten it. Today's schools must make sure that the entire learning community is technologically competent.

The International Society for Technology in Education, which involves several professional organizations and governmental/corporate sponsorship, realized the need for technology standards to facilitate educational reform. Today's students must be prepared to cope with technology, yet many of their teachers have not been trained in this area.

ISTE's technological standards for students are designed to be incorporated across curricular lines; they work as tools to help students learn cognitively and affectively. The library media teacher can collaborate in several ways to implement ISTE's standards; they reinforce information literacy standards very well. There are six competency strands:

1. *Technology operations and concepts.* Library media teachers can reinforce computer skills through one-on-one coaching, guidesheets, and posted Web tutorials. They can also instruct classes of students, staff, and parents. To keep the community current, library media teachers can use "push" technology, forwarding good Web sites that come across the computer screen as well as good articles in their fields of interest. Youngsters can get specialized, in-depth training in technology operations through tech aide programs coordinated through the library media center.

2. *Social, ethical, and human issues.* Probably the most effective approach in this area is to model behavior. Does the media center have legal copies of all software? Does the library media teacher help students critically evaluate Web sites for their social and ethical implications? Does the media center post copyright notices and point out the need

for citing sources when students produce multimedia projects? Does the library media teacher help students and parents understand the reasoning behind acceptable use policies, not just enforce signatures? Does the library media teacher collaborate with the school community to address Digital Divide issues to ensure that all students have equitable access to technology? Does the library media teacher work with teachers to provide appropriate technology accommodations for students with special needs?

3. *Technology productivity tools.* When producing documents for the school community, the library media teacher should demonstrate how each technology tool can "ratchet up" the product's quality: attractive layout and complementary images in newsletters; sortable databases of books or local resources; use of predictive capabilities of spreadsheets for budgets or demographic trends; combination of media for effective presentations; documentation preservation of videotaped speakers or events; in-depth connections through hot-linked Web pages. As with technology operations, use of productivity tools can be optimized through learning aids and just-in-time help. Library media teachers can also help the school community collect good examples of productivity tool utilization.

4. *Technology communication tools.* Electronic communication should be a mainstay activity of library media teachers: e-mail, listservs, groupware, real-time conferencing, and Web pages. Library media teachers should emphasize the timeliness and proactivity of these channels. Web pages should be maintained regularly and change in response to community needs. E-mail should be used to advance committee work as well as announce media center activities or call attention to overdue equipment. Does the media center allow students to e-mail their peers or their teachers about assignments? Can students download articles from the Internet and then e-mail them to their home stations? Does the media center have videoconferencing access, and does the library media teacher plan co-curricular video activities with the student body or other school community members? Library media teachers can advise video and digital image clubs in which students can learn how to use these communication tools and provide service for the school; library media teachers can also work with local cable or other communication businesses to help the school community gain access to these outlets and explore careers in these areas.

5. *Technology research tools.* This standard highlights core media center service and resources. It also highlights the issue of owning versus accessing information and the issue of evaluating sources. In pre-technology days, the library media center's collection was carefully selected (theoretically, at least), so the school community just needed to know if the information was useful for a particular topic and intellectually accessible. Now library media teachers have the responsibility of teaching others how to carefully evaluate and select sources from a world of possibilities. Instructional design changes with the incorporation of technology, and library media teachers provide a broad perspective on appropriate research tools and procedures,

along with experience in educational technology. Library media teachers can also teach parents how to get involved with their children's research efforts—without doing their work. The concept of family-engaged research effort is very powerful and can extend the concept of schoolwide initiatives.

6. *Technology problem-solving and decision-making tools.* Of course, locating and accessing information is just a beginning step. Library media teachers should work with students and teachers to ferret out the meaning of the information, analyze it, interpret it, and make it their own. This is where lesson design planning comes into play as the library media teacher and teacher decide the best way for students to organize information for meaning: Should students develop a class database of plants? Should small collaborative groups produce simulated newspapers to capture the essence of a historical period? Should individual students e-mail their legislators about current local controversial issues that they have researched?

Along with these student-based standards, ISTE developed technology standards for teachers. This set builds on the students' list. Two of the student standards also have a teacher "spin:" assessment and evaluation in terms of matching learning activities to student needs and use of productivity and communication tools to enhance professional practice. Two others focus on the teaching profession: planning and designing learning environments and experiences and teaching/learning and the curriculum. These standards cut to the heart of media center programs and enable library media teachers to advocate these standards.

Library media teachers have always had a variety of resources from which to choose to meet a student's specific needs, and they have always needed to organize these resources to optimize access and minimize duplicative effort. They have worked with teachers and students to diagnose and satisfy needs at any moment. As classroom teachers venture into these functions, they cannot and should not start from scratch or try to duplicate the library media teacher's work; they have neither the training nor the time. Rather, classroom teachers can complement the library media teacher's strengths through their in-depth knowledge of content and student skills. It should be noted that this kind of collaboration also affects scheduling of classes and student groups as well as planning time with staff. Coordination of time, facilities, and control itself can pose a threat for each constituency, so the incorporation of technology highlights the need for interpersonal and communication skills.

Institutional support and coordination underlie success in implementing the ISTE standards, be they for students or teachers. ISTE realized this early on, and simultaneously developed essential conditions for implementing these standards, with a focus on teacher preparation. Universities are called upon to coordinate efforts closely with their communities, and library media teachers can play a significant role here. Ten of the essential conditions follow:

Shared vision: Library media teachers can work with the rest of the staff to determine the vision for teacher support relative to technology, particularly for first-year teachers.

Access: Library media teachers can provide teacher work areas with Internet access (and access to other technologies). They can also circulate technology equipment.

Skilled educators: Library media teachers can model the effective use of productivity, communication, and instructional technology tools.

Professional development: In collaboration with the school community and local groups, library media teachers can train and coach colleagues and provide information about continuing education opportunities and links to Web tutorials.

Technical assistance: Library media teachers can help troubleshoot technical problems. They can also work with colleagues to train and coordinate student tech teams who can help staff. Library media teachers can also suggest preventative care tips for technology.

Content standards and curriculum resources: The library media center can maintain a print and online professional collection. Together with faculty, library media teachers can develop the collection of (and access to) worldwide electronic resources. In an academic community spirit, information literacy standards and technology standards can be aligned with content standards.

Student-centered teaching: Library media teachers can work with teachers to ensure that technology-rich resources and services meet student-specific needs. Information literacy processes can be used as an instructional/learning model.

Assessment: Library media teachers can locate and provide access to technology-enhanced assessment tools, such as online diagnostic exercises, rubrics, and statistical software. They can also help assess student work and design interventions or lesson modifications to improve student success.

Community support: Library media teachers can link the school community with the community at large through communications about local events and issues, databases of local resources, grantsmanship, and networking efforts.

Support policies: Library media teachers can help hire technologically competent staff and mentor new teachers.

Technology Close Up

This workshop is targeted to library media teachers who want to help the school community become more technologically adept. The emphasis is on using technology to model the learning itself.

Training through Online Technology

- *During this session we will:*

  – Examine characteristics of ADULT LEARNERS,

  – Look at ONLINE TRAINING METHODS, and

– Discuss creating TRAINING .

- *Who are ADULT LEARNERS?*

    – Are self-directed

    – Have experience

    – Are real-world based

    – Want applications

    – Are interactive

    – Need repetition

    – Have limited time

- *Obstacles to Adult Learning:*

    – Fear of criticism

    – Negative past training

    – Competing priorities

    – Bad pacing

    – Lack of control

    – Lack of time

- *Implications for Technology:*

    – Make it USEFUL.

    – Make it HANDS-ON.

    – Let people SHARE.

    – Build in social contact.

    – Deal with mixed ABILITIES.

    – Consider variety of LEARNING STYLES.

    – Have DEADLINES.

    – Be PREPARED.

    – Be SUPPORTIVE!

- *Planning Training—Overall Factors:*

    – Outcomes

    – Audience

    – Format

    – Time frame

    – Facilities

    – Resources

    – Administration

    – Evaluation

- *Determining Outcomes:*

    – Who is the audience?

    – What will they be able to do?

    – Under what conditions?

    – To what degree?

    – How will the training be applied??

- *Planning for the Audience:*

    – Who is the audience?

    – What do they already know?

    – What should they know by the end?

    – What barriers exist?

    – What learning styles must be addressed?

- *Planning Format:*

    – Classroom presentation

    – Manuals

    – Job aids

    – Computer-based training

    – Videotape

    – Online

    – Distance learning

- *Planning Time Frame:*

    – Number of times

    – Length of session

    – Pacing

    – Follow-up

- *Setting up Facilities:*

    – Space

    – Room arrangement

    – Equipment

    – Electricity

    – Communications tools

    – Supplies

    – Food

    – Human needs

- *Selecting Resources:*

    - Human: who will teach?

    - Training aids

    - Reference tools

    - Handouts

    - Recording devices

    - Base on the task and the learner

- *Planning Administration:*

    - Needs assessment

    - Publicity

    - Registration

    - Set-up

    - Funding

    - Publishing

    - Evaluation

- *Evaluation Factors:*

    - Content: difficulty, theory/practice, useful

    - Delivery: format, pace, sequence, clarity, equipment necessities

    - Resources: handouts, aids

    - Online and followup

- *Training Tools:*

    - E-mail

    - Listservs/newsgroups

    - Realtime chat

    - Online documents

    - Web tutorials

    - Course packaging

    - CD-ROMs

- *Presentation:*

    - Communicate main ideas in a short time.

    - Have a strong opening and closing.

    - Use visual aids.

    - Burden is on the trainer!

    - Example: Reading on information literacy.

- *Question and Answer:*

  - Know your topic.

  - Know the type of questions to ask.

  - Watch the time.

  - Stimulate thinking.

  - Use with uninformed audiences

  - Involve the learner.

  - Example: threaded discussion about Internet use.

- *Small Group Discussion:*

  - Give clear direction.

  - Read attentively.

  - Group heterogeneously.

  - Give quick feedback.

  - Guide, don't influence.

  - Report out.

  - Example: incorporating CD-ROMs into the curriculum.

- *Demonstration/Practice:*

  - Keep demo simple.

  - Let learners practice.

  - Keep learners involved.

  - Give immediate feedback.

  - Provide guidesheets and references.

  - Example: desktop publishing.

- *Case Study/Simulation:*

  - Focus on problem analysis.

  - Encourage questions and different solutions.

  - Relate topic to real life.

  - Requires much development time.

  - Example: lab troubleshooting.

- *Buddy Coaching:*

  - Time intensive

  - Good for specific and need-to-know basis

  - Use for guidesheet development

  - Encourage partnership relationship

  - Example: planning lesson /student activity

- *Online Tips:*

    - Be organized.
    - Define terms and give examples.
    - Highlight critical elements.
    - Use concrete, active examples.
    - DO things.
    - Check for understanding.
    - BE PREPARED!

- *Tips to Involve Learners:*

    - Have interactive interface with blanks to fill in.
    - Include discussion forums.
    - Use games/simulations/role play.
    - Include hands-on practice.
    - Incorporate projects.
    - Encourage e-mail.
    - Keep pace up.
    - HAVE FUN!

PUTTING IT ALL TOGETHER

15

Because the school library media center program may involve a variety of group partnerships, careful coordination of efforts is essential. In addition, each partnership should be assessed in terms of its effectiveness in meeting desired goals. The library media teacher can optimize partnerships to meet media center goals as well as contribute to the goal of the school community: to help each child.

Coordination versus Control

One partnership is good, two are better, but what happens when the library media center collaborates with a myriad of individuals and groups, each with different agendas? There is a fear that the bottom may fall out, and that the real reason for all of these collaborations, student success, will disappear. The fact of the matter is that the library media teacher can no longer control all the elements. The traditional media center, in which the library media teacher knew where every book was on the shelf and in which hands it resided at any time, is gone, as is the time when the library media teacher knew every single book or item in the media center.

Technology does help, because the library media teacher can keep track of the materials more closely and can tell who has checked out the book—and who forgot to check the item out, because the security alarm rang at the time. Still, the media center cannot control all the information that it now can access because of technology.

That same problem exists for libraries that foster partnerships. Once others are involved, they have a stake in the results and so want part of the input and authority as well. Otherwise, a partnership does not really exist; instead, a hierarchical entity comes into being. Control does not equal effectiveness. In a closed system, control is possible and, indeed, desirable. The classroom teacher who cannot maintain a safe learning environment will have trouble teaching. The library media teacher must manage resources thoughtfully to provide efficient service. But most educational systems are open-ended, both because the clientele change every year (or more often) and because resources and outside factors constantly change. Total control is impossible, but coordination is feasible within one's sphere of influence.

The focus must remain on the school's ultimate mission: to prepare young people for lifelong learning, self-realization, and responsible citizenship. Partnerships can be viewed in terms of how they advance—or detract from—that goal. The approach is rather like keeping one's eye on the steady horizon ahead instead of on the rushing cars alongside. This "macro" approach enables the library media teacher to measure partnerships individually and in relation to each other. For example, the library media teacher can take each of the principles of the media center program as detailed by AASL and describe how each partnership affects each objective. To help organize this assessment, the library media teacher can create a database by type of partnership (see Table 15.1).

Table 15.1. Sample Partnership Evaluation Database

	Learn/Teach	**Information Access/Delivery**	**Program Administration**
Teachers			
Support staff			
Administrators			
Students			
Families			

The database can be detailed to capture subgroups within the categories (e.g., grade level, academic discipline, committee, etc.), and can also be developed on a broader level, such as community stakeholders, with each row representing a particular group to capture the specifics (see Table 15.2).

Table 15.2. Sample Partnership Evaluation Database

	Learn/Teach	**Information Access/Delivery**	**Program Administration**
School community			
Civic groups			
Private entities			
Organizations			
Higher education			

By examining such a database, the library media teacher can see where partners naturally align or even overlap. In some cases, those possibly duplicative groups might want to collaborate to maximize benefits with the minimum outlay. To uncover that detail, another dimension should be added to the database (see Table 15.3).

Table 15.3. Sample Partnership Evaluation Database with Goals

	Goals	**Input**	**Processes**	**Output**	**Impact**
Teachers					
Support staff					
Administrators					
Students					
Families					

Each of these categories may be subdivided as well:

Goals: that group's mission, goals, objectives

Resources: human, material, financial, facilities/space

Processes: what people do, what technologies do

Output: products produced and used, services used

Impact: the degree to which the intended population changes/learns

The library media teacher can analyze what resources are available for each partner and how those resources are deployed. By overlapping Tables 5.1 and 5.2 and Table 5.3, the library media teacher can start to see interesting trends and ways that partnerships can be optimized to reach similar goals. By adding each partner's goals, the library media teacher may also see conflicting goals, the reason why resources are redirected that do not help the library media center. On the positive end, serendipitous relations may come to light through this analysis.

This perspective still does not capture the essence of a partnership because it uses as its raison d'être the library media program. Although such a perspective seems reasonable for the library media teacher to carry out the program for which he or she is responsible, it does not address the media center's contribution to other partners' agendas. As library media teachers reach out to understand other groups' priorities, they may find that they have more in common than they thought. For example, both the athletic director and the library media teacher may be trying to help students analyze information and might both use spreadsheets to organize data; they can reinforce each other's objectives when helping students within their own environments.

A more accurate representation should include the library media center alongside the other groups, incorporating the school's overriding goals as well as each partner's goals. In each case, the goals remain the touchstone. This representation also makes obvious the rationale for mutually supportive goals throughout the school community: Resources can be used more effectively and efficiently.

So what does all of this have to do with control? Rather than trying to control partners, library media teachers should concentrate on coordinating the partnership *itself* so possible conflicts in goals, resources, and processes can be resolved to mutual satisfaction. When the partnership itself is in good shape and people respect each other and communicate effectively, all parties can act responsibly within their specific environments and facilitate each other's agendas. When problems do arise, partners can focus on that one aspect rather than worry about the rest of the partnership's existence. That one problem can be isolated and controlled, then set back into its context to improve the overall effort. In other words, when the "macro" system is in place, the "micro" management of specific issues works well.

Evaluation

By now it should be obvious that evaluation should occur throughout partnerships, from identifying potential collaborators to determining whether the groups have met their goals and should be disbanded—or redirected. In each case, partners should define the desired outcome and identify criteria by which to measure success. Measurement itself is not enough, however; as the adage goes, "Weighing the pig more often doesn't make it gain weight." Judging the discrepancy between actual evidence and the ideal outcome enables partners to address the gaps and develop appropriate interventions to bridge those gaps. The previous section provides the foundation for evaluation because it emphasizes the two main factors to assess: the ends and the means. How well are goals attained and how effective are the means?

The process of evaluation involves the following steps:

1. Define the need for the evaluation.
2. Plan the evaluation.
3. Collect the data.
4. Analyze the data.
5. Report the results.
6. Plan the next action.

Different types of evaluations have different objectives and ask different questions (Hanson, 1998, p. 44):

- *Needs assessment* describes present reality, identifies problems or gaps, and asks what is needed and how needs can be addressed.

- *Process evaluation* examines the way the project is planned and implemented and asks how the collaboration works.

- *Formative evaluation* measures project progress and asks how to improve.

- *Impact evaluation* measures change and asks what difference the effort made to the targeted audience.

- *Summative evaluation* examines project quality and asks about its continued worth.

All evaluations should address the following questions:

- *Who?* Who will evaluate? Who will be evaluated? Will the assessor be an outsider or insider?

- *What?* What will be evaluated? Input/resources? Process? Output/product? Impact? The more specific the target, the easier to assess it.

- *How?* How will the evaluation be done, that is, using what instrument(s)? Who will choose the instrument?

- *Where?* Where will the assessment be done? At school? In the community? Face to face? Online?

- *When?* At what point(s)? Will the evaluation be a needs assessment, a formative process, or a summative analysis? How long does it take to locate or develop the assessment tool? Is it necessary to schedule the assessment? How long does it take to administer the assessment tool? How often should the assessment be done? How quickly can results be determined?

- *Why?* Why is the evaluation being done: to measure impact, to examine the partnership itself, to determine student success, to provide redirection, to develop interventions? The more specific the reason, the easier it is to plan the evaluation.

The Milken Exchange on Educational Technology describes seven dimensions for gauging progress, with an emphasis on incorporating technology into the learning community (Lemke & Coughlin, 1998). By asking the right questions, partners can develop a meaningful evaluation process that can optimize impact.

1. *Learners.* Are students fluent technology users? Do they demonstrate breadth and depth of knowledge? Are their learning experiences relevant to real life? Does technology help motivate student learning? Do students understand the benefits and drawbacks of technology?

2. *Learning environments.* Is learning contextualized? Do standards and curriculum reflect the real world? Does the school culture foster educational improvement? Is technology accessible? Is information literacy modeled throughout the learning community?

3. *Professional competency.* Are staff technologically competent? Can they incorporate technology to improve learning? Do they use technology to improve their own practice?

4. *System capacity.* Does the community embrace a compelling vision and clear expectations? Is technology aligned with a comprehensive long-term plan? Does the infrastructure supply needed capacity to implement the plan? Does leadership analyze the learning community systematically?

5. *Community connections.* Are community partners involved through-out the school's improvement plan? Have all potential collaborations been identified and developed? Do all partners have a clear understanding of the plan and expectations? Is communication effective?

6. *Technology capacity.* Are technology infrastructure and equipment available to all in support of the learning community? Is connectivity adequate to carry out learning activities? Is technical assistance adequate and timely? Are users satisfied with the level and operation of technology? Are facilities capable of supporting needed technology?

7. *Accountability.* Have goals and benchmarks been established? Are data collection and analysis processes effectively done? Is decision making driven by data? Are results communicated broadly and effectively?

Of course, these questions should fit the environment in which learning communities exist. Besides the ubiquity of information and technology in society, other issues laid out in Chapter 1 affect education: global economics, changing demographics, the Digital Divide, and new insights into education itself.

Assessment Instruments

Naturally, the reason for the evaluation determines the choice of assessment instrument. For example, to measure student achievement, formal tests (norm-referenced or criterion-referenced), portfolios, presentations, or products may be used. Questionnaires, interviews, and journals can capture attitude. To measure interaction, assessors can observe practice or analyze documents (e.g., meeting minutes and threaded discussion).

When choosing the type of assessment instrument, partners should also consider the context of the assessment:

Cost: Should professional forms be developed or acquired? Are Scantrons needed? Can assessments be done by an outside contractor? If done on-line, must the developer be paid?

Availability: Can an appropriate instrument be located? Are there time, staff, or cost restrictions involved? Should an instrument be developed?

Size: Should everyone assess or be assessed? What sampling percentage and method will produce valid results?

Scope: What is the impact of the evaluation: Does it affect one function, or does it have overarching consequences? High-stakes evaluations can be stressful—and require extremely careful planning. Usually all stakeholders who are affected by the evaluation should participate in its planning and analysis.

Skills: What skills does the assessor need to do the task (e.g., read, use e-mail, conduct clinical observations, conduct interviews)? Do assessors need training? Should assessors be "calibrated" so the data will be consistent across personalities? Can volunteers be used?

Legalities: Do partners have permission to use the measurement tool? Is parental permission needed to assess students or to have students assess? Are issues of confidentiality and privacy addressed adequately?

Culture: How will those people who are assessed react? Will they introduce bias? Are unobtrusive measurements more reliable? Do groups hold certain beliefs about evaluation? Do groups fear or welcome change?

Each assessment instrument has its strengths and weaknesses. Table 15.4 lists some of these characteristics.

Table 15.4. Characteristics of Assessment Instruments

Method	Strengths	Weaknesses
Records analysis	Unobtrusive, exists, can be repurposed	Confidentiality issues, criteria-sensitive
Observation	Open-ended, natural setting	Requires training, presence may skew behavior, only measures data for that time
Interview: group	Interactive, open-ended, shows group dynamics	Misses individual differences, may push conformity, question-sensitive, language issue
Interview: individual	Open-ended, can capture in-depth, interactive	Time-consuming, labor-intensive, requires training, question-sensitive, language issue
Interview: telephone	Interactive, space-independent, less intense/intimidating	Requires training, data may be hard to capture, hang-ups, biased sample (unlisted numbers, lack of phone, language)
Questionnaire	Self-administered, easy to conduct, cost can be low	Self-reporting may be biased, issues of language/literacy, need to test questions
Test	Standardized, easy to conduct	Might not fit population; issues of language/literacy

Several of these instruments may use technology, such as online tests, surveys, and interviews. In some cases, privacy issues may be addressed more satisfactorily using technology. Remote access may expand participation. However, equity issues may arise because of limited access to equipment or limited experience with the technology.

Some data already exist: student records, meeting minutes, sample work, policies, publications, and so forth. In some cases, evidence of everyday practice is needed, which may be captured on camera or camcorder, observed directly, or recorded via journals or logs. In other cases, groups should be asked to provide input; for this, tests, surveys, questionnaires, focus discussions, and interviews may be used. Whenever possible, partners should try to locate existing, validated instruments rather than try to create one from scratch. Not only does instrument develop take time and skill, the instrument also has to be tested to ensure its reliability and validity.

Whatever measurement tools are used to evaluate, they must be reliable (measure consistently) and valid (measure the right things). Measurement tools may be quantitative (i.e., numerical) or qualitative (i.e., descriptive). In general, evaluation should include multiple measurement tools assessed by multiple constituents; for example, to measure the effectiveness of online communication between partners, both partners should do the assessment, which can include the number of e-mail messages sent, the number of replies, the time lag between messages and action, content analysis of the messages, and self-assessment of communication effectiveness. Results can then be triangulated to uncover discrepancies in perceptions or measurements. These differences can be very valuable; for example, if one partner thinks the relationship is fine and the other one thinks the relationship is dysfunctional, the evaluator can disaggregate the data to discover possible reasons for the discrepancy, then build on that information to initiate frank discussion between the two partners.

Analysis of the data collected from these instruments gets at the heart of the process. A first skim of the material should cause evaluators to ask: "What patterns emerge?" "What discrepancies appear?" It is important to look at the data from different angles to get a richer picture of the underlying factors. For this reason, partners should disaggregate the data in appropriate ways: socio-economic, gender, age, length of time in the partnership, position/title, location, and so forth.

Even before collecting the data, partners should consider which factors might affect results because this information enters into the decision of which instrument to use. If, for example, "time" is mentioned repeatedly, then it may be a key element in shaping partnerships. Do some constituents have more difficulty in time management or scheduling? Does the school year calendar affect time allocation? By digging into the data, evaluators may conclude that joint staff planning time is crucial for project success, or they may recommend that all staff have e-mail accounts so they can collaborate asynchronously. Because collaboration reflects a complex and interdependent set of behaviors, skills, and knowledge, it may be difficult to ferret out one outstanding issue. One way to help sort out the details is to develop a spreadsheet or chart of the possible trends and factors, noting the evidence to back the analysis. Another method is to use concept mapping or another form of graphic organizer. Sophisticated evaluators can take advantage of technology by using online surveys and exporting the data into database files to be analyzed using statistical packages such as SPSS. These structuring methods can prevent evaluators from jumping to premature conclusions; the mantras "Show me the evidence" and "No recommendation before its analysis" should guide decision making.

Timely reporting of the data and the analysis improves the evaluators' reputation. Those who participate in the assessment process need the reassurances of followup and the sense that the evaluators care about the target groups. Sharing the information also builds the knowledge base and keeps people involved. Evaluation should make a difference. Not all data should be reported to everyone, however. "Just-in-time" release of information on a "need to know" basis works well. Most groups prefer clear, simple presentations of the basic facts; a graphical representation provides an easy way for the audience to interpret the information. In some cases, reporting may have political or group culture ramifications. If so, all efforts should be made to keep the report objective and neutral. In any case, reporting should be accurate and professional looking. Normally, a formal report includes an introduction with background information, a description of the evaluation process, data analysis, and the action plan. The means of reporting vary; a variety of communications channels should be used to ensure that all interested partners—and the community in general—get the needed information. Typical venues are public meetings, local media, and telecommunications. As with other public relations efforts, the message should be tailored to the target audience and the medium and to the objective of the report. For example, preliminary recommendations may take the place of an action plan if the objective of the report is to elicit comments and inform future decision-making efforts.

Of course, the main reason for the evaluation is to make reasoned decisions about the partnership and its efforts. In effect, the planning process recycles—or, rather, spirals. Sometimes referred to as the cycle of inquiry, evaluation undergirds school improvement. The focus on partnerships points out the need to reflect on process as much as on product.

Redirection

Remember the speaker who lost the audience, but still kept droning on with his original speech? His impact was negligible and negative. The same thing can happen with partnerships that are not mutually responsive to needs: within each group, between them, or outside their organizations. So beyond scheduled assessments, partner leaders should keep their ears to the ground to sense unrest or stagnation. Particularly in short-term projects or beginning partnerships, constant attention to group dynamics facilitates timely interventions that can lead to stable conditions and progress for the task at hand.

In some cases, the original project might not accurately reflect the community's needs. Changing the emphasis can make all the difference. For example, the school might want to integrate technology into the curriculum and so go to great efforts to partner with local businesses to buy current equipment. The library media teacher might install great software and network the system, in partnership with tech experts, in anticipation of increased use. When use of the library media center doesn't change, the library media teacher may need to work with teacher groups to determine what underlies the situation. Perhaps teachers have not transformed their lessons when thinking about technology, but have just added tech "icing." The project must refocus on collaborative teacher training, either using in-house expertise or partnering with district or community sources.

In other cases, the project is completed and the goals have been met. Partners may feel let down and at loose ends at this point. Rather than lose momentum, partners have a number of options to pursue. First, for the sake of the local community and for education in general, they should disseminate information about their process and product. In so doing, they may develop new partnerships or get new ideas for ways to extend their work. Even between partners, new ideas for collaboration may occur in related or completely untouched areas. For example, business partners that started out donating machines may want to tutor students or offer training for faculty. A successful videoconferencing with city hall may parlay into student internships. Partners may want to call for a hiatus or regroup after an intense project and should follow their instincts in such matters, because otherwise they may burn out or feel manipulated rather than proud. Partners often have many other irons in the fire that they may have neglected because of the collaborative task at hand. Sensitivity to each other's agendas helps to set a positive tone for future cooperative projects.

If partners want to extend their relationship they should plan accordingly, taking the following factors into consideration. In each case, partners should develop criteria and agree on processes by which to make and support their decisions (Otterbourg, 1986, p. 277):

> *Partners:* Should new partners be invited to join? Should present membership be reconfigured?
>
> *Leadership:* Should leadership change if the goal changes? Should the type of leadership—or the leader's role—change?
>
> *Needs:* What issues now need attention? What gaps exist?
>
> *Goals:* What are the new goals? Should present goals be modified?
>
> *Resources:* What resources exist to address needs and goals? What new resources are required?
>
> *Staffing:* Should staffing be adjusted, or training be done?
>
> *Finances:* Can existing funds be repurposed? Is fund-raising needed?
>
> *Policies:* Do present policies cover the extension or adjustment? Should new policies be developed? Should forms be created or modified?
>
> *Communication:* How will changes be communicated? Should communication channels be upgraded or expanded?

Maximizing the Impact

One of the attractions of partnerships is their combined power to create something neither party could do alone, bringing unique perspectives and resources together to innovate a better future for the school community. Partnerships usually require commitment and effort. Ownership comes with the belief that the goals—and process—are worth the investment. Passion for the task motivates partners to do their best and optimize their impact. Sometimes potential partners have little time or resources so may just commit to a supportive role and the use of their names to attract other partners. As long as both parties realize the limitations of such collaboration, that level can be tolerated, particularly if there exists a possibility that a deeper partnership may grow in the future. Limited but defined collaboration is preferable to situations in which partners pledge great support but deliver very little. Such disappointments merit careful and honest investigation into underlying issues; either the problem is solved or the partnership as a whole must be redirected or terminated for a time.

For the most part, though, partners usually want to achieve their goals effectively. In fact, they hope to maximize their impact both for their own reputation as well as for the sake of the group they are helping. They can approach this goal from two angles: internal and external. That is, they can affect the partnership and its processes optimally, or they can disseminate information to affect others to a greater degree. In either case, they should identify their core activities, use data to monitor their work, and involve all stakeholders in the process.

Normally, partnerships seek to implement their plan, to have their constituents accept and apply their strategies. Several factors facilitate such adoption, and technology can play a role in optimizing each one (Lindquist, 1979, p. 54):

Relative advantage: The plan reflects the best solution of several possible choices. Graphic organizers can help visualize options. Spreadsheets can help groups predict consequences of economic decisions. Computer models can show alternatives.

Complexity: The simpler the innovation and the easier it is to understand, the more likely it is to be adopted. Tables and graphs can simplify main points.

Compatibility: How well does the plan align with current practice and culture? If existing technology can be used as is or repurposed easily, then adoption is facilitated.

Trialability: Can groups pilot-test the innovation without having to commit to it totally from the start? Technology models can use key concepts.

Reversibility: Can the group stop the plan without risk to the community's current status? Technology helps trace steps, document activity, and back up procedures for easier recovery.

Divisibility: Can the plan be implemented in smaller steps or by phases? Project management software can clarify tasks and deadlines.

Communicability: How easily can information about the plan be conveyed? Telecommunications and the Internet specifically can facilitate in-house discussion as well as external dissemination and interaction.

Adaptability: Can the plan or model be customized to the site? This factor helps different types of groups adopt the same general plan yet keep their own integrity. Templates can provide a guiding structure with areas for individualization.

Cost: The lower the cost, the more groups can participate. Technology can be used effectively to merge data and allocate resources effectively.

Realization: How quickly will the community see the plan's benefits? Statistical packages speed up data analysis. Telecommunication speeds up information dissemination.

Risk: The lower the risk, the more likely the adoption. Technology can help isolate cases for easier testing. Back-ups of data lower the chances of lost information.

When a number of partners work on a project, individual entities may embrace parts of the plan before other parts, and to different degrees. For example, if a group already leans toward innovation, it may adopt the plan earlier. Early adopters risk more—to their benefit or dismay. If the innovation benefits the target group, others will be more likely to join, and the risk-taking group strengthens their reputation. If problems arise, either other groups will shy away from the plan or they will try to "get the kinks out" before they implement it themselves. On the other hand, late adopters may miss out on maximum funding and benefits. Generally, to start implementing the plan, groups should have a choice of various ways to get involved; flexibility and decentralization help. Just-in-time telecommunications, dynamic databases and Web pages, and online training offer several channels for growth. However, to follow through with the entire plan, group leadership should facilitate change through clear central goals, expectations, and reinforcement. Technology can help in this process by standardizing data with relational databases and hyperlinked Web sites. With healthy partnerships, groups can shore each other up through risky times so no one will fail significantly.

Six Sigma offers a useful model to ratchet up those factors by looking at the processes behind the innovations. In the 1980s Motorola started an aggressive quality improvement and business strategy to optimize profits. This infrastructure, called Six Sigma, provides a mindset to motivate and improve organizational culture. This set of strategic tools has been adapted by many businesses and can be adapted for partnerships. Basically, the partnership is analyzed as a system of processes with inputs and output within an environment of suppliers and customers (i.e., the community). The goal is to process better, faster, and at less cost. To achieve this cost-efficiency goal, Six Sigma identifies three levels of leaders: experts (most likely the heads of each group), masters (usually the partnership steering committee or chairs of sub-task groups), and leadership teams (significant committees). Experts provide the broadest perspective and sense of coordination, masters head main components, and leadership teams model effective collaboration within a specific objective or institution. Regardless of rank, partners *prioritize* processes and determine who is responsible for these processes. Then they detail each process's characteristics (steps and flow, evaluation method, sources of variability, source and extent of control of these processes). With these data, partners can then optimize variables and measure the improvement of the entire process.

To illustrate this approach, consider classroom and library media teacher partners who want to keep students from cheating on research reports. They look at the research process and identify those variables that may lead to cheating: task identification (e.g., comparing two different subjects leads to less cheating than describing one subject), locating information (e.g., stopping with encyclopedias or using just one or two sources), extracting the information (e.g., downloading an article rather than taking notes), presenting information (e.g., debating an issue leads to less cheating than writing a five-page persuasive report). Partners optimize each variable, then measure the impact. As can be imagined, student cheating should decrease and student information literacy skills should increase.

When partners experience success in their efforts, especially as student performance improves, they typically want to share the information. For the sake of the greater educational and social community, they also have a responsibility to explain how their model works so others can replicate their efforts and help more partnerships. The typical approach is one-way communication: publications and presentations to relevant groups. Some tips to optimize the message include presenting a clear and simple message, use of graphics. presentation tools such as PowerPoint to make the point obvious, using evidence and logic, and being flexible. If one approach does not reach the audience, try another method. The same project can be customized to address the specific needs of each audience and thereby broaden the impact. Two-way personalization deepens the impact because the disseminator can link networks together. Particularly if the project communicators have a strong reputation, their connections can attract others and supply a growing number of partners. Of course, the real action occurs at the local level, where groups can adapt the project model to solve their own problems. The original project leaders can help these folks identify their own needs, collect and analyze data, and work collaboratively. In this scenario, all parties must be receptive and attentive.

Technology offers worldwide dissemination and connections. Partnerships can start by posting documents on the Internet. On a more formal basis, they can submit project information to services such as ERIC to share with the educational world. Groups can also act proactively by posting findings on listservs, conducting online "chats" and videoconferences, and developing videotapes about their efforts for broadcast purposes. With the decreased cost of CD-R burners, partners can develop a hyperlinked electronic portfolio of their project, complete with video clips, and create a CD-ROM that can be cheaply duplicated and disseminated. With the myriad of communication channels available these days, partners would be remiss not to take advantage of the opportunities to spread their good message, increase their impact, and broaden their partnership networks.

For the Sake of a Child

All of this work! Is it worth it? Hopefully, collaboration broadens people's perspectives and opens doors to opportunities impossible to realize alone. By merging and complementing resources and skills, partners create a stronger social safety net as well as a means to higher achievement. In these days of constant change, partnerships provide a stable mechanism to adapt to fluctuating pressures and constituents. Technology undergirds these efforts by providing a variety of means to gather, analyze, archive, and share information across platforms, partners, and space.

Students come and go, and the school community has a social and intellectual obligation to help students within their sphere of influence. Each intervention affects a child's future—and the future of the community at large. Every child deserves the best education and the best future. Partnerships bind the child to the community as the child binds the community together.

Close Up

Table 15.5 illustrates the principles of library media programs (AASL & AECT, 1998) that deal with elements of collaboration. Assessment tools are identified and impact on student learning is delineated to help library media teachers examine their practice critically.

Table 15.5. Library Media Program Partnership Assessment

Principle	Assessment Instrument	Impact
Information literacy	Scope-and-sequence information integrated across the curriculum literacy instruction, student work, assignments, syllabi, outcomes/graduation requirements, library media center documents/Web page	Students link research skills across curriculum
Collaborative planning and teaching	Assignments, planning documents, planning time, curriculum development policies	Consistent messages about information literacy, higher levels of learning
Support of diverse learning styles	Lesson plans, teaching aids, student work, observation	Equitable access to resources, higher rate of student success
Collaborative collection development	Survey, recommendations, bibliographies, syllabi, policies	Resources meet school community needs
Link to the larger community	Meeting minutes, survey, Web page, databases, interview, survey	Greater school-community collaboration, increased school support
Library media center supports school	Web page, planning documents, mission statement, observation, committee documents, events	Library media center integrated more, school improves
Library media center strategic planning	Planning documents, meeting minutes, survey, observation	Library media center and school aligned, more resources/services to meet school community needs
Administrative support	Budget, staffing, administrative documents, school policies, strategic plans, interview	Greater ability to meet school community needs
Ongoing staff development	Workshop documents, Web pages, observation, survey	Improved instruction, higher student achievement
Clear communication	Publications, presentations, telecommunications, survey, observation, interview	Greater understanding of library media center, improved collaboration

REFERENCES AND ADDITIONAL READING

Abramson, J., & Stulberg, L. (1997). *The Internet and community*. Aspen, CO: Institute for Information Studies, the Aspen Institute.

Alexander, B. (2000, May). Illinois promotes equal access to libraries through partnerships. *OCLC Newsletter*, 31–33.

American Association of School Librarians & Association for Educational Communications and Technology. (1998). *Information power: Guidelines for effective library media programs*. Chicago: American Library Association.

American Educational Research Association. (1995). *School-linked comprehensive services for children and families*. Washington, DC: U.S. Department of Education.

American Institutes for Reform. (1999). *An educators' guide to schoolwide reform*. Arlington, VA: Educational Research Services.

American Library Association. (2000a). *Community partnerships toolkit*. Chicago: American Library Association.

American Library Association. (2000b). *Decide tomorrow today: Libraries build sustainable communities*. Chicago: American Library Association.

American Library Association. (2000c). *Libraries & the Internet toolkit*. Chicago: American Library Association.

Annenberg Institute on Public Engagement for Public Education. (1998). *Reasons for hope, voices for change*. Providence, RI: Annenberg Institute for School Reform.

Bajjaly, S. (1999). *The community networking handbook*. Chicago: American Library Association.

Barber, J., et al. (2000). *Parents as partners*. Berkeley, CA: Gems.

Baron, R., & Greenberg, J. (1989). *Behavior in organizations*. 3rd ed. Boston: Allyn & Bacon.

Barth, S. (2000, December). The power of one. *Knowledge Management*, 30–36.

Benton Foundation (1996). *Buildings, books, and bytes: Libraries and communities in the digital age*. Washington, DC: Benton Foundation.

Berger, C. (2000). *Public and school libraries: Issues and options of joint use facilities and co-operative use agreements.* Sacramento: California State Library.

Berger, E. (1995). *Parents as partners in education.* 4th ed. Englewood Cliffs, NJ: Prentice-Hall.

Blake, F., et al. (1985). *Forging coalitions for the public good.* Chicago: American Library Association.

Bolt, D., & Crawford, R. (2000). *Digital Divide: Computers and our children's future.* New York: TV Books.

Boston Consulting Group. (1997). *Benefiting from advanced telecommunications and information technology in the Bay Area.* San Francisco: Bay Area Council.

Bradburn, F. (1999). *Output measures for school library media programs.* New York: Neal-Schuman.

Brown, J., & Guguid, P. (2000). *The social life of information.* Boston: Harvard Business School Press.

Buckley, F. (1999). *Team teaching: What, why, and how?* Thousand Oaks, CA: Sage Publications.

Building a community of learners: It's just good teaching. (2000). Portland, OR: Northwest Regional Educational Laboratory.

Building strong connections between schools and communities. (2000). Philadelphia: Annenberg Institute for School Reform. http://www.aisr.brown.edu/community/index.html

Building successful partnerships: A guide for developing parent and family involvement programs. (2000). Chicago: PTA.

Burke, J., & Prater, C. (2000). *I'll grant you that.* Portsmouth, NH: Heinemann.

California Association of Library Trustees and Commissioners. (1998). *Trustee tool kit for library leadership.* Sacramento: California State Library.

California Education Technology Task Force. (1996). *Connect, compute, compete.* Sacramento: California Department of Education.

California Library Association. (1998). *Kids Connect @ California Libraries.* Sacramento: CLA.

California School Library Association Technology Committee. (1998). *Technology planning and grant resources information packet.* Sacramento: California School Library Association.

Caywood, C. (Ed.). (1995). *Youth participation in school and public libraries: It works.* Chicago: Young Adult Library Services Association.

Center for Children and Technology. (1998). *The benefits of online mentoring for high school girls: Telementoring young women in science, engineering, and computer project.* New York: Center for Children and Technology.

Center for Innovative Learning Technologies. http://www.cilt.org

Children's Partnership. (2000). *Online content for low-income and underserved Americans: The Digital Divide's new frontier.* Santa Monica, CA: Children's Partnership.

Children's Partnership, National PTA, & National Urban League. (1998). *The parents' guide to the Information Superhighway: Rules & tools for families online.* Santa Monica, CA: Children's Partnership.

Clyde, L. (2000). *Managing infotech in school library media centers.* Englewood, CO: Libraries Unlimited.

Community Technology Centers' Network. http://www.ctcnet.org

A compact for learning: An action handbook for family-school-community partnerships. (1997). Washington, DC: U.S. Department of Education.

Conte, D. (1997). *The learning connection: Schools in the information age.* Washington, DC: Benton Foundation.

De Klerk, Gerta (Ed.). (1998). *Virtual power: Technology, education and community.* Long Beach: Pacific Southwest Regional Technology in Education Consortium.

DiSessa, A. (2000). *Changing minds: Computers, learning, and literacy.* Cambridge, MA: MIT Press.

Earle, J., & Kruse, S. (1999). *Organizational literacy for educators.* Mahwah, NJ: Lawrence Erlbaum Associates.

Educational Research Service. (1998). *Parent involvement.* Arlington, VA: ERS.

Educational technology. (2000). Washington, DC: Eisenhower National Clearinghouse for Mathematics and Science Education. http://www.enc.org

Eisler, R. (1999). *Tomorrow's children: A blueprint for partnership education in the 21st century.* Boulder, CO: Westview Press.

Ellis, S., & Craven, J. (2000). *The virtual volunteering guidebook.* Palo Alto, CA: Impact Online.

Epstein, J., et al. (1997). *School, family, and community partnerships: Your handbook for action.* Thousand Oaks, CA: Corwin Press.

Everhart, N. (1998). *Evaluating the school library media center.* Englewood, CO: Libraries Unlimited.

Fagnano, C., & Werber, B. (1994). *School, family and community interaction.* San Francisco: Westview Press.

Farmer, L. (1994). *Leadership within the school library and beyond.* Worthington, OH: Linworth.

Farmer, L. (1997). *Training student library staff.* Worthington, OH: Linworth.

Farmer, L. (1998). *Cooperative learning activities in the library media center.* 2d ed. Englewood, CO: Libraries Unlimited.

Farmer, L. (1999). *Partnerships for lifelong learning.* 2d ed. Worthington, OH: Linworth.

Farmer, L. (2000a). *An examination of the state of school libraries and the relationship to perceptions held by school site personnel towards library media program principles.* An unpublished report to the Scholarly and Creative Activities Committee, California State University, Long Beach.

Farmer, L. (2000b, September).The powers of management. *The Book Report,* 15–16.

Farmer, L., & Fowler, W. (1999). *More than information: The role of the library media center in the multimedia classroom.* Worthington, OH: Linworth.

Fitzpatrick, K. (1998). *Program evaluation: Library media services.* Schaumberg, IL: National Study of School Evaluation.

Fixing our schools now! (2000). Washington, DC: U.S. Department of Education.

Flowers, H. (1998). *Public relations for school library media programs.* New York: Neal-Schuman.

Forum on the future of technology in education. (2000). Washington, DC: U.S. Department of Education. http://www.air.org/forum

Furger, R. (2000, Fall). Bringing schools & services together. *Edutopia,* 4–5.

Giving in America: Toward a strong voluntary sector. (1975). Washington, DC: Commission on Private Philanthropy and Public Needs.

Greater Bay Area Library Council. (1998). *Connections: Opening Greater Bay Area Libraries to Students and Teachers.* San Francisco: GBALC.

Hancock, V. (1995, September). Information literacy, brain-based learning, and the technological revolution: Implications for education. *School Library Media Activities Monthly,* 31–34.

Hanson, S. (1998, September). Evaluation: A tool for continuous improvement. *Knowledge Quest,* 44–45.

Hellriegel, D., Slocum, J., Jr., & Woodman, R. (1995). *Organizational behavior.* 7th ed. Minneapolis: West.

Hernon, P. (1990). *Evaluation and library decision making.* Norwood, NJ: Ablex Publishing.

Hill, P., Campbell, C., & Harvey, J. (1999). *It takes a city: Getting serious about urban school reform.* Washington, DC: Brookings Institute.

Hubbard, J. (1997). *Dynamics of Alliances.* Aurora, CO: Mid-continent Research for Education and Learning.

International Center for Communications. (1997). *Building smart communities.* San Diego: San Diego State University.

International Society for Technology in Education. (2000). *National educational technology standards for teachers.* Eugene, OR: International Society for Technology in Education.

Johnson, S. (1997). *Interface culture: How new technology transforms the way we create and communicate.* San Francisco: Harper.

Katz, J. (1998). *Losing ground bit by bit: Low income communities in the Information Age.* Washington, DC: Benton Foundation. http://benton.org/Library/Low-Income

Kearney, C. (2000). *Curricular partner: Redefining the role of the library media specialist.* Westport, CT: Greenwood.

Koulopoulos, T. (2000, December). The edge of knowledge. *Knowledge Management,* 12.

Lance, K., Rodney, M., & Hamilton-Pennell, C. (2000*). How school librarians help kids achieve standards: The second Colorado study.* San Jose, CA: Hi Willow.

Learner-Centered Principles Work Group of the American Psychological Association's Board of Educational Affairs. (1997). *Learner-centered psychological principles.* Washington, DC: American Psychological Association.

Lemke, C., & Coughlin, E. (1998). *Technology in American schools: Seven dimensions of progress, an educator's guide.* Santa Monica, CA: Milken Family Foundation. http://www.mff.org/edtech

Libraries for the Future. (1998a). *Common ground.* New York: Libraries for the Future.

Libraries for the Future. (1998b). *Communities and libraries: A dialogue.* New York: Libraries for the Future.

Liebert, D. (2000, November). Co-opting the cooperating teachers. *Principal,* 36–38.

Lindquist, J. (1979). *Increasing the impact of social innovations funding by grantmaking organizations.* Battle Creek, MI: W. K. Kellogg Foundation.

Loertscher, D., & Woolls, B. (1998). *Information literacy: A review of the research.* San Jose, CA: Hi Willow.

MacIntyre, G. (1997). *Active partners: Education and local development.* North York, ONT: Stoddart.

Marin County Public School Libraries. (1999). San Rafael, CA: Marin County Grand Jury. http://grandjury.marin.org/1998gj/library.html

Maslow, A. H. (1968). *Toward a psychology of being.* New York: Van Nostrand Reinhold.

Mayor's Office of Community Development. (1998). *Amended 1998 action plan support for San Francisco's community development block grant program; emergency shelter grant program and home investment partnership.* San Francisco: City and County of San Francisco.

McCook, K. (2000, September 1). Reconnecting library education and the mission of community. *Library Journal,* 164–165.

McLester, S. (2000, November 30). Learning gets some technical support. *Los Angeles Times,* T8.

Molnar, A., & Morales, J. (2000, October). Commercialism@Schools. *Educational Leadership,* 39–44.

National Academy of Science. (1995). *Reinventing school: The technology is now.* Washington, DC: National Academy of Science.

National Association of Partners in Education. http://www.napehq.org

National Education Association. (2000). *1999–2000 Resolutions.* Washington, DC: NEA. http://www.nea.org/resolutions.

The National Network of Partnership Schools. http://www.csos.jhu.edu/p2000/

National Reading Panel. (2000). *Teaching children to read: An evidence-based assessment of the scientific research literature on reading and its implications for reading instruction.* Atlanta: National Institutes of Health.

National School Network. (1999). *Electronic collaboration: A practical guide for educators.* http://www.lab.brown.edu/public/ocsc/collaboration.guide

National survey of American adults on technology/national survey of American kids on technology. (2000). Washington, DC: National Public Radio. http://www.npr.org/programs/specials/poll/technology

National Telecommunications and Information Administration. (2000). *Falling through the net: Toward digital inclusion.* Washington, DC: U.S. Department of Commerce. http://www.ntia.doc.gov

North Central Regional Educational Laboratory. http://www.ncrel.org

Northwest Educational Technology Consortium. http://www.nwet.org

Northwest Regional Educational Laboratory. http://www.nwrel.org

Necroponte, N. (1995). *Being digital.* New York: Knopf.

Odasz, F. (1999, Spring). Big visions from small village schools. *Edutopia,* 5–6.

Orange County Task Force for School Libraries. (2000). *Libraries lead learning.* Costa Mesa, CA: Orange County Department of Education.

Oregon Parent Information & Resource Center. http://www.nwrel.org/pirc

Otterbourg, S. (1986). *School partnership handbook.* Englewood, NJ: Prentice-Hall.

Owens, R. (1995). *Organizational behavior in education.* 5th ed. Boston: Allyn & Brown.

Parentech: Partnering in a digital age. (2000). Oak Brook, IL: North Central Regional Educational Laboratory. http://www.parentech.org

Partnership for Family Involvement in Education. (1998). *Employers, families and education.* Washington, DC: Government Printing Office.

Peto, E., et al. (1998). *Tech team.* Worthington, OH: Linworth.

Recognizing excellence in afterschool programs for young adults. (2000). Chicago: American Library Association.

Rockwell, R., Hawley, M., & Andre, L. (1997). *Parents and teachers as partners: Issues and challenges.* Stamford, CT: Wadsworth.

Sagor, R. (1993). *How to conduct collaborative action research.* Alexandria, VA: Association for Supervision and Curriculum Development.

Schein, E. (1970). *Organizational psychology.* 2d ed. Englewood Cliffs, NJ: Prentice-Hall.

Schon, D., Anyal, B., & Mitchell, W. (Ed.). (1998). *High technology and low-income communities.* Cambridge, MA: MIT Press.

Schools as centers of community: A citizen's guide for planning and design. (2000). Washington, DC: U.S. Department of Education.

Schuler, D., & McLelland, J. (1999). *Public space in cyberspace: Library advocacy in the information age.* New York: Libraries for the Future.

Scott, C., & Jaffe, D. (1991). *Empowerment: A practical guide for success.* Menlo Park, CA: Crisp.

Secretary's Commission on Achieving Necessary Skills (SCANS). (1991). *What work requires of schools: A SCANS report for America 2000.* Washington, DC: Government Printing Office.

Senge, P. (1994). *The fifth discipline: The art and practice of the learning experience.* New York: Bantam Doubleday Dell.

Six Sigma for manufacturing and non-manufacturing processes. (2000). Colorado Springs, CO: Air Academy Associates.

Slavin, R. (2000, December). Putting the school back in school reform. *Educational Leadership, 22–27.*

Snyder, T. (2000). *Getting lead-bottomed administrators excited about school library media centers.* Englewood, CO: Libraries Unlimited.

Strong Families, Strong Schools. http://eric-web.tc.columbia.edu/families/strong

Technology: Indicators of quality information technology in K-12 schools. (1999). Schaumberg, IL: National Study of School Evaluation.

Technology applications for bilingual education and English as a second language. (1997). Albany: New York State Education Department.

Tello, J., & Weber, L. (1993). *Developing public library service for youth.* Los Angeles: Los Angeles Public Library Young Adult Services.

21st Century Community Learning Centers Program. (1999). *A guide to continuous improvement management.* Washington, DC: U.S. Department of Education.

Umbach, K. (1998). *Computer technology in California K-12 schools: Uses, best practices, and policy implications.* Sacramento: California State Library

U.S. Department of Commerce. (1999). *How access benefits children: Connecting our kids to the world of information.* Washington, DC: U.S. Department of Commerce.

U.S. Department of Education (1998). *Family involvement in children's education: Successful local approaches.* Washington, DC: U.S. Department of Education.

U.S. Department of Education Office of Educational Research and Improvement and the American Educational Research Association. (1995). *School-linked comprehensive services for children and families: what we know and what we need to know.* Washington, DC: U.S. Department of Education.

U.S. Department of Education Office of Educational Technology. (2000a). *E-learning*. Washington, DC: U.S. Department of Education. http://www.ed.gov/Technology/elearning/index.html

U.S. Department of Education Office of Educational Technology (2000b). *Tool kit for bridging the digital divide in your community*. Washington, DC: U.S. Department of Education. http://www.ed.gov/Technology/tool_kit.html

U.S. National Commission on Excellence in Education. (1983). *A nation at risk*. Washington, DC: Government Printing Office.

Van House, N., & Childers, T. (1993). *The public library effectiveness study*. Chicago: American Library Association.

Virtual volunteering project. (2000). Austin: University of Texas. http://www.serviceleader.org/vv/

Warns, A., Underberg, T., & Cothrel, J. (2000, December). Active management 101. *Knowledge Management*, 74–75.

Winn, P. (1991). *Integration of the secondary school library media center into the curriculum*. Englewood, CO: Libraries Unlimited.

Wood, K., & Dickinson, T. (Ed.). (2000). *Promoting literacy in grades 4-9*. Boston: Allyn & Bacon.

Yap, K. (1999). *Evaluating whole-school reform efforts*. Portland, OR: NorthWest Regional Educational Laboratory.

INDEX

Technology, 19, 23–44, 48, 51–52, 54, 57, 63,
65, 74, 76, 78–80, 90–93, 98, 107–8, 113,
115, 120, 125–26, 129, 133, 135–37,
142–44, 146, 152, 155, 158, 161, 164,
166–67–76, 181–82, 189
Technology plan, 15, 26, 156–60, 164, 166,
181
Technology specialist, 75, 158
Technology standards, 26, 36–43, 65, 99, 146,
168–71
Telecommunications, 23–24, 32–33, 48, 51,
64, 67, 76, 78, 80, 98, 107–8, 111, 116,
120–1, 124, 126, 132, 135, 140, 147,
156–57, 164, 169, 187–89. *See also*
Communication; Internet
TeleVillage Project, 120
Television, 93, 116, 127, 133–34, 136, 138, 166,
169, 189
Template, 33, 187
Tenure, 97
Tests, 182–83
Texas Community Networking Guide, 126
Textbooks, 49, 146
T.H.E. Journal, 135
Threaded discussion, 24, 33
Time, 23, 29, 134, 170, 173, 184, 186
Timeline, 136
Training, 34, 36–43, 65–67, 72–73, 76, 78, 81,
83–84, 90–91, 94–95, 107–9, 119–22,
124–26, 131–32, 136, 154, 157, 159,
163–65, 168, 171–76, 182, 185–86
Transportation, 89, 91, 93

Union lists/catalogs, 109
Unions, 62, 77
United States Department of Education, 26,
103, 120
United States Department of Transportation,
120

United States National Commission on
Excellence in Education, 154
United States National Commission on
Library and Information Science, 128
Universities, 36–43, 74, 97–103, 119–20, 136,
153–54, 178
University of California Los Angeles, 121
University of Missouri, 110

Values, 50, 53, 62, 70, 163
Vermont, 136
Video games, 24
Videoconferencing, 32–33, 48, 109, 143, 164,
166, 169, 186, 189
Videotapes, 25, 34, 51, 55, 66–67, 73, 76, 81,
83, 93–94, 100, 107–9, 120, 127, 132–34,
136, 141, 146, 149, 156, 169, 183, 189
Vision, 63, 82, 153, 156, 170. *See also* Mission
Visuals, 29–30, 187
Volunteers, 60, 82–85, 87, 90–95, 119, 121–22,
124, 127, 135, 164, 166, 182

Warns, A., 35
Web sites, 13–5,19, 24, 36, 51, 63, 76–77,
90–94, 106–7, 109, 117, 119–20, 125–28,
132, 135–37, 139–40, 142–43, 146, 149,
155–56, 161, 164, 168–69, 171, 174, 188,
190
WebQuests, 34, 155
Whitefoord Community Program, 119
Wood, K., 82
Word processing, 24
Workshops, 5, 21–22, 54, 94, 124, 126, 133,
141, 154, 161, 164, 171–76
World Wide Web, 33–34, 165. *See also*
Internet
Writing, 150

Young Women's Technology Club, 126
Ysleta District, 82